THE SUPERPROMOTER

THE SUPERPROMOTER

The Power of Enthusiasm

Rijn Vogelaar

Director, Blauw Research

Translated by Peter de Wolff

Published in Dutch as "De Superpromoter; de kracht van enthousiasme", van Duuren Management, 2009

Published 2011 by
PALGRAVE MACMILLAN

Palgrave Macmillan in the UK is an imprint of Macmillan Publishers Limited, registered in England, company number 785998, of Houndmills, Basingstoke, Hampshire RG21 6XS.

Palgrave Macmillan in the US is a division of St Martin's Press LLC, 175 Fifth Avenue, New York, NY 10010.

Palgrave Macmillan is the global academic imprint of the above companies and has companies and representatives throughout the world.

Palgrave® and Macmillan® are registered trademarks in the United States, the United Kingdom, Europe and other countries.

ISBN: 978–0–230–28509–5

This book is printed on paper suitable for recycling and made from fully managed and sustained forest sources. Logging, pulping and manufacturing processes are expected to conform to the environmental regulations of the country of origin.

A catalogue record for this book is available from the British Library.

A catalog record for this book is available from the Library of Congress.

10 9 8 7 6 5 4 3 2 1
20 19 18 17 16 15 14 13 12 11

Printed and bound in Great Britain by
MPG Group, Bodmin and Kings Lynn

CONTENTS

CONTENTS

FIGURES AND TABLES

FIGURES

TABLES

PREFACE

There are times when I'm running a research company; sometimes I'm a table tennis player and at other times I compete in poetry slams. Apart from this, I'm a father, husband and – like everybody else – at times I'm consumer, client, patient, member of the public and traveler. The thing I've learned in life is that, to me at least, there is one thing that is highly important whatever role I happen to be occupying. It is enthusiasm. Anything I do is made different by the presence or absence of enthusiasm: mine influences how I am able to function; the enthusiasm of others can really get me going. We all know this: enthusiasm can be wonderfully infectious!

How people exercise influence on each other was always of interest to me. Back then it influenced my decision to study Social Psychology. Having duly completed my studies and done my share of applied life-exploration in the bars and pubs of Amsterdam, Rotterdam and Leeds, I did my military service in the Royal Navy. During my stint at the Ministry of Defence I was employed as a behavioral scientist, and from there I moved on to Blauw Research, which is a Dutch research company. My research involved customer relationships and employee motivation, and I got involved with research into company reputation, new-product launches and advertising campaigns. Having had all of these different experiences, I have come to a certain insight that I would like to share with you here.

WHAT IS MY INSIGHT?

That it is the transfer of enthusiasm from one person to another that lies at the foundation of a company's success. It is the force that fuels employee motivation and people's personal development. People can be infected with enthusiasm for all kinds of things, whether products, companies, brands, jobs, and so on. When others share in the enthusiasm, positive things start to happen. Conversely, if people's enthusiasm fails to ignite others, leaving them indifferent or even provoking resistance, it will soon be extinguished.

Enthusiasm was a recurring topic in hundreds of interviews my colleagues and I have conducted. Literally thousands of consumers answered our questionnaires, the employees from more than a hundred companies were interviewed, and the levels of enthusiasm existing among large public groups have been measured. Everywhere we ran into the influence of enthusiasm: on how people do things and of course on how they feel about doing those things. At the direct and personal level I've also experienced the compelling force of enthusiasm, from our clients, for example, but also from my colleagues at Blauw Research. As long as enthusiasm is greasing the wheels, all rolls along smoothly; but as soon as that level of enthusiasm runs low, everything becomes an uphill struggle. I always thought it odd, but I have not been able to discover much scientific research into enthusiasm's influence; it gets no thematic treatment in the management literature that I've seen. However, the existing literature did cover for example studies of copycat or, as it's sometimes called, Herd behavior, word-of-mouth behavior, as well as social networks, Web 2.0, Human Resource Management, and the role of influencing. There are any amounts of books for sale that attempt to explain company or marketing success stories. And yet my many conversations with entrepreneurs, marketing people and communication experts have only served to strengthen my conviction that the influence of enthusiasm lies at the foundation of success.

This book will be introducing you to the *superpromoter*. Superpromoters personify the power of enthusiasm; they are the enthusiasts who in sharing their enthusiasm around infect others with it. We come across superpromoters all the time. They are the customers making recommendations that bring in new customers; they are the employees who get really involved and thereby change the working environment; they are the members of the public who stand up to defend some government policy they strongly believe in. They are the backers of companies or government bodies, the people acting behind the scenes to ensure its success, whether that means sales growth, building a good reputation or creating more effective management. Of course some people end up as superpromoters more often than others, but all of us will be at one time or another. It is fair to say that everyone allows themselves to be influenced by a superpromoter sometimes. For most, it is comforting when someone we trust and take seriously tells us what to do, what to pick, what to go for... that way we don't have to reinvent the wheel each time. And it is a generally acknowledged fact that we are apt to make superior choices when we allow ourselves to be influenced by enthusiastic superpromoters. All of us also need superpromoters to give us self-confidence and to stimulate our creativity. They can show us what we are good at and urge us on to develop our talents further. Keep in mind: not only are superpromoters enthusiastic about products or companies, they can also be enthusiastic about us as individuals!

For example, while I was honing my skills as a performing poet – no doubt my most vulnerable role – it was the influence of superpromoters that made the difference. Without them, I would never have made it as a poet, I'm sure it would have all fizzled out in a hurry. The earliest poem I wrote during my last year in High School was inspired by my first lesson in poetry appreciation. After class I decided to risk writing one of my own; it was a sonnet on longing for the end of term. Looking back, today I have to confess that it wasn't exactly a masterpiece. Nonetheless, my teacher reacted with enthusiasm and encouraged me to publish my poetry in the school's newspaper. Soon after, during my first performances, it was the reaction from the audience that gave me enough confidence to continue working on my chosen art form: performing poetry onstage. When I submitted my poetry to publishers for evaluation, their positive feedback prompted me to publish a collection of my poetry. The first superpromoters of this collection rewarded me with a 'best-debut' prize; and just before he died, that most loved Dutch writer and poet, Simon Vinkenoog, wrote an inspired and most poetical blurb for the back cover. There is no denying this did wonders for the sale of my little book, turning it into one of the best-selling poetry collections published at that time – not that this means a great deal in Holland: total sales were around 1,500 copies! The point is, these superpromoters, during key moments in my budding career as a poet, handed me sufficient confidence to carry on. They helped me to get other people interested in my poetry. In becoming a table tennis player and in my work as a researcher, superpromoters played a comparable role.

Probably you'll have had very much the same kind of experience. We all need a little encouragement from time to time...someone to encourage you to push on, regardless of what others might have to say. This book also would never have seen the light of day without superpromoters. Like good friends, they spent time looking at my efforts critically and firing up my own enthusiasm as I was making progress. That is why this book is dedicated to them! The Superpromoters!

FOREWORD DUTCH VERSION

SUPERPROMOTION

I have great respect for those who realise things that are greater than themselves: entrepreneurs, record holders, composers and, for example, writers. At an early stage I got the opportunity to read the manuscript of the book that you have before you now. Rijn Vogelaar, accomplished leader of Blauw Research, has outdone himself.

Aside from the daily hustle and bustle that comes with running a company and a family, Rijn found the time and energy to write a book about something that had preoccupied his mind for a while. "Why is it that some organizations or products become so popular over a short period of time and stay that way?" Surprised that the existing knowledge of marketing did not come up with a satisfying answer, he started his research. In this book Rijn describes the invisible mechanisms of social networks and he analyses the exact impact of influence. He uses the most recent marketing insights and brilliantly connects them.

Rijn concludes that behind the complex social reality of recommendation behavior and opinion leadership lies a key that has been missing in the way we think. And with the insight to that key he creates an almost completely fresh way of approaching marketing.

The superpromoter and his polar opposite the "anti promoter", emerge unmistakably as the most important, but yet invisible, forces behind the rise or fall of a product or company. A vast potential that, until now, has not been utilized by the industry.

He also agonizingly reveals that the current methods organizations use to improve customer satisfaction are ultimately counter productive. Creating, identifying and shaping superpromoters is the one new and clever way of marketing, according to Rijn. And I concur. Personally I think these new insights can lead to great implications for product development, marketing, management and research.

This is an impressive piece of avant-garde thinking, that might even put the Netherlands on the map within this field. I have said it before, sometimes people do things that are greater than they are. This book is a pleasure to read, and it will lead to new and useful insights for your business. I also wish it will make you an enthusiastic promoter of the superpromoter concept. In my case it has done just that.

Kees de Jong
Superpromoter and CEO of SSI and
co-founder of Blauw Research

FOREWORD

Hats off to Rijn Vogelaar! Well done...from this moment on, a plain recommendation will be just that...plain! Without enthusiasm, without passion, a recommendation is merely an opinion that may or may not be followed. Only a Superpromoter delivers!

I'll be honest, I started reading this book with a level of skepticism, thinking it would be yet another of the dozens of book out regularly preaching the importance of including customer insights into our business and how indeed the voice of our customer matters. But I must admit, I was quite blown away by so many different concepts Vogelaar throws at us.

From the perfect trifecta in how a Superpromoter impacts the world, to the more advanced Odilia concept, *The Superpromoter* is a joy to read.

When we meet enthusiastic people who can influence the world around them, share their enthusiasm about their experiences, they are the billboard and ads that we hope our marketing campaigns will yield toward market growth. That's the power of a Superpromoter.

In the movie *Untouchables*, Robert De Niro playing Al Capone has a speech that talks to the significance of enthusiasm. "man becomes preeminent, he's expected to have enthusiasms. Enthusiasm..Enthusiasm...What are mine? What draws my admiration? What is that which gives me joy? Baseball!..."

The words, admiration and joy in the speech, the way they convey the active experience are the make up of what Vogelaars' Superpromoters are all about...

I've spent a decade and a half driving customer centric change in major organizations, and I am now a Superpromoter of SuperPromoter. We hear acronyms all the time , but the ones in the book such as AM (animosity metric), SSM (Social sharing metric) and of course, as previously mentioned ODELIA should be on your list of "must know" terms.

The Superpromoter is game-changing! I know it's made me re-think my strategy!

Suhail Khan
Vice President Philips International
Head of Customer Experience and
Market Driven Innovation

1

INTRODUCTION

Suppose for a moment that you're the lead singer of a well-known rock and roll band...every night performing at overflowing sports arenas and being cheered by your enthusiastic fans. One night, you get this live connection to your public when they all start singing along with you. The energy flowing from an audience that's going wild pushes the band on to greater heights, each single band member is playing as never before and as a band you all reach some kind of harmonic perfection. Both band and audience are aware that they have participated in something very special and unique. At the end of a stunningly brilliant concert everybody leaves, still buzzing with excitement. The next day, at work, in school, everybody who attended the performance is talking about the great experience they had; their friends are all seriously miffed that they weren't there, but will be buying the CD and making sure they won't miss the next concert.

A ROCK STAR'S LIFE

Our rock star has no need for this book. Obviously he'll already have a good grasp of the principles being described.

Here is how it works. He performs for fans of his music: they are his encouragement in writing new songs and the reason he's on tour all the time, going from one concert to the next. It looks like a fair exchange: he is giving his audience an unforgettable experience and they are bringing in scores of new fans that have been infected with their enthusiasm. This chain of events allows our lead singer to do what he likes doing best, which is to make music.

Those of us not confronted daily with audiences going wild, however, might find this book to be of some interest. Most of us, unfortunately, never hear the sound of cheering fans. In fact, we're much more likely to be listening to customer complaints, dissatisfied colleagues, acidic journalism or frustrated citizens, to name a few examples. Like the squeaky wheel, the louder the complaint, the more attention it gets. Most companies and organizations are focused on the things that go wrong. Quality control systems and improvement programs are entirely focused on the stuff that goes off the rails. Those members of the public that are in disagreement with their government about something, or are dissatisfied with their living conditions and are loud about it, will be getting lots of attention. If you're a consumer buying a lemon or the victim of some awful service you'll be given plenty of opportunity to get heard. Sometimes it feels as if the complainers are running things; just take a look at the examples the Web will turn up for you. Today, there even are corporate hate-sites, specifically created as a forum for complaining about a given company. Examples would be www.ihatedell.net (Dell), www.amexsux.com (American Express) or www.paypalsucks.com (Paypal). Complaining, it seems fair to say, is a widely accepted phenomenon throughout every segment of today's society.

Having said that, it is not generally true that those who complain about everything and who are never enthusiastic about anything are the ones who make change happen. Progress stems from people who can identify opportunities instead of problems; people who have the ability to become really enthusiastic about the possibilities that life throws up now and again. These are the people capable of being constructively critical instead of being destructive. These are the people who can infect others with their enthusiasm and win them over to their side. These are the people who help to make our world a bit nicer and a bit better.

Yet, why does it often seem as if many companies are basically trying to perform classical music for a rock and roll audience? The answer is actually quite simple. They invited the wrong audience, or they are performing in the wrong auditorium. A rock star would never be dragging his audience in by the hair, lock them up in a concert hall or bother them at a time when they just don't want to listen to his music. He's not on an ongoing quest for improvements that are designed to appeal to the average listener. He'll be concentrating on his biggest fans and be playing the songs that get them most excited. He will entirely ignore those people who do not care about his music. No artist would be able to keep up playing night after night to an audience that doesn't care.

Incidentally, in my role as a market-researcher I can also feel guilty of making this mistake. Properly considered, the main purpose and focus of market research is to deliver bad news. Whether it's an advertising campaign that was cancelled during the test-phase, or new product defects that get analyzed to death, or complaining customers who get the spotlight or dissatisfied colleagues who are given a soapbox from which to ventilate their frustrations. For all intents and purposes market research is really the business of flagging concerns: the red flag gets raised when something is going wrong. It is no surprise that most marketing people, ad agencies and other professional types consider market research to be a pain in the neck, if not a bit lower. And that's quite understandable. We've all seen it happen many times: along comes the marketing department, full of enthusiasm about a new product, or with a cool idea for a marketing campaign, only to find that their enthusiasm hardly ever gets corroborated by market research. Most market researchers delivering the bad news will have encountered all five stages of the grief process (denial, anger, bargaining, depression, and sometimes, acceptance) in these situations. What this suggests is that if research, however well conceived and executed, can meet such resistance; it is not realistic to expect it to contribute to making any great change going forward. That is why the time has come for us to try a new approach, not just in how we do market research, but also in our marketing, communication, even in our overall company management methods.

From now on, let us no longer put the emphasis on what the complainers are telling us, but let's clear the floor for the enthusiasts. Particularly for those people who are advertising their enthusiasm from the rooftops and are infecting their surroundings with it: they are the superpromoters. These are the people who can make us happy by telling us about all the things that are going well. These are the people who can also be very good at explaining how best to take advantage of new trends and how to leave our competition far behind us. But, that requires us to develop a new way of seeing things. Instead of putting so much of our energy into those whose weighty complaints will cause them to fall of the stern of their ship, companies and other organizations ought to be much more focused on what is happening up at the bow. That's how to set sail with all your fans onboard and on course to discover new horizons. The message I would like to pass on is that it is time to change course...the ship is ready to cast off...*all aboard that's coming aboard...?*

THE PROMISE CONTAINED IN *THE SUPERPROMOTER*

In writing *The Superpromoter*, I have tried to set out my ideas about the influence of enthusiasm on companies, about the people who work there and about you and me, ordinary people. The thinking behind these ideas has been based on experiments used in social psychology, recent management and marketing literature and also on research conducted by Blauw Research. I would like to think that, upon reading *The Superpromoter* it will become very clear who your superpromoters are, and what they could mean to you. Superpromoters are responsible for sales growth, or for having motivated employees. *The Superpromoter* will show you the inside workings of superpromoting, probably something you already have an instinctive feel for, but don't quite recognize at the conscious level. From there it's only one little step more to learn how to recognize your own superpromoters, how to develop them further and collaborate with them effectively.

I would hope that readers of this book will start thinking about the superpromoters in their immediate environment. Who are the superpromoters that motivate you? Are you one yourself? Who are the superpromoters that are important to you? *The Superpromoter* also tells you how you can find them and how to put them to work for you, which is also when it starts getting a bit more fun. After all, listening to what a superpromoter has to say is a pretty nice thing. We all like to hear other people talking enthusiastically about something, even if we don't really have any connection to what they are being enthusiastic about. Then think how you'd feel when they are being enthusiastic about you, or the company you work for. Just imagine that this superpromoter is your client or someone who works with you. That's when you start getting an idea of how our rock star must be feeling every day. Superpromoters are a source of energy and inspiration.

Superpromoters: Why would you like to know them?

They...
...produce turnover growth
...determine your reputation
...teach you what is good for you
...motivate you and your staff
...join in your thinking process; they are co-creators
...are responsible for more results for less money!

What this book is trying to do is to show entrepreneurs and new product developers how superpromoters are their greatest source of inspiration in developing successful products. Company executives will get a clear demonstration how superpromoters are responsible for the growth of their company's turnover and reputation. Managers and Human Resource professionals will have an opportunity to discover how employee motivation and personal development are largely dependent on the superpromoters that can be found among clients and colleagues. In fact, superpromoters among your colleagues should be nurtured and involved in all the important choices that need to be made. In *The Superpromoter* I will attempt to show to communication and marketing experts that mass communication is ineffective if superpromoters aren't enthusiastic about it. Furthermore, superpromoting offers a way of saving on marketing and communication expenses while achieving superior results. Government policy makers will be made aware that they can have supporters among an enthusiastic public. One of the aims of *The Superpromoter* is to convince the reader that, both at the personal and business level, they will experience a great deal of pleasure from the superpromoter. That's the promise! Now it's time to take a closer look.

2

STARTING FROM SCRATCH: LET ME TELL YOU SOME MORE . . .

DEFINITION AND DESCRIPTIONS

The Superpromoter is all about the influence of enthusiasm and enthusiasts. I mean the type of enthusiasm that produces word-of-mouth behavior; the enthusiasm that is infectious on first contact. Although enthusiasts are the people who spread it around, we will be training our sights on one particular breed of enthusiast: the superpromoter. We've created a definition of a superpromoter and this chapter will provide descriptions of the various guises in which you may encounter them.

The definition is basically very simple.

> *A superpromoter is an enthusiast who shares and wears their enthusiasm, and influences other people by spreading it around.*

Superpromoters play a key role in their social networks simply because, whether consciously or not, they are infecting others with their enthusiasm. We don't always realize this, but superpromoters enable us to make faster decisions and do not force us to think everything through first. We would be exhausted if first we had to carefully consider each decision or analyze everything to death. Now, this does not mean that superpromoters always exercise their power over us in the same manner. Some act as role models, thereby causing those around them, their social environment, to assume their attitudes. Others might have expertise in a specific area and be asked for advice all the time. And then it might be their superior social skills that give superpromoters their influence. Most of the time it seems to be a combination of all of these factors that plays a role.

It wouldn't be right to think of superpromoters as being pushy, irritating or hot air blowing windbags who are trying to shove their opinions down your throat. Throat shovers, we all know from painful experience, have a strictly limited impact. The enthusiasm of superpromoters is sincere; there is something they want to share with you because they believe you could benefit from it. This is also what makes them believable, increasing the likelihood of you taking up their recommendations. Of course superpromoters enjoy giving advice to other people; like anybody else, they feel appreciated when their enthusiasm meets with a favorable reaction.

Because they come in all shapes and sizes, superpromoters do not always represent the voice of authority, nor are they necessarily the most popular guys on the block. By their nature and personality some people are constantly superpromoting, while others only superpromote specific things or in some specific circumstances. Similarly, being a superpromoter in one social network does not automatically mean you'll be one in other networks. We shall be taking a closer look at the different forms superpromoters can take during the remainder of this chapter.

Having sketched an outline of the basic shape of superpromoters, let's try to make them come more alive in our imagination by adding a couple of specific descriptions of superpromoters. These examples haven't been made up, they actually represent real people, and of the kind that you or I could meet every day.

Leon is an MBA who has been reading the *Financial Times* since he was a student; he still reads it from cover to cover every evening when he gets home. He even has it forwarded to him when he goes on his holidays. Leon actively promotes the virtues of the *FT* at work, and among his circle of friends he shares his enthusiasm freely. He likes to talk about the editorials over lunch and often cites the newspaper as his source of information during discussions with people. At work two of his colleagues have become subscribers and almost all of his friends have had subscriptions to the *FT* for a while.

Bart likes to wear the Copa label. Because he is an avid football fan he likes to wear shirts sub-labeled 'designed by Copa', as that way he won't be a banner for a particular football club. The appeal of the Copa label is that their fashions give a light and humorous touch along with a great fit. Most wearers have the experience that the design of the shirts will often form the start of a nice conversation, especially at the football club. These shirts know how to make a statement. For example, the one printed with a copy of *The Last Supper*, but with well-known players substituting for the more traditional faces. Bart has been asked several times where he gets his shirts, and even though he doesn't really have a stake in other people wearing the same shirts, several people at the club, and some of his relatives have now also started wearing the Copa label.

Nicole likes cars. Although they don't mean much to her husband, she likes to keep up with all the latest developments in the automotive world. For several years now Nicole has been an avid Audi fan, something she is not shy about. Nicole is the type of person who, if she spots one of the new Audi models on the road, will point them out to her passengers while giving them a rundown of the car's performance stats. Fortunately for her, Nicole and her husband can afford an Audi for themselves and her husband lets her make the car decisions.

THREE ESSENTIAL CHARACTERISTICS IN CLOSE-UP

Superpromoters have to meet three criteria. First, they must be enthusiastic about something; second, they have to broadcast this enthusiasm to the world and third, they

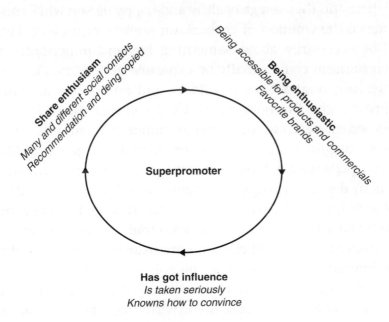

Has got influence
Is taken seriously
Knowns how to convince

Figure 2.1 Characteristics of the superpromoter

have to be able to exert influence on others with their enthusiasm.

A superpromoter will demonstrate the following three characteristics:

1. A superpromoter is enthusiastic
2. A superpromoter shares this enthusiasm
3. A superpromoter has influence

Let us for a moment take a look at the origins of enthusiasm, the several ways in which it can be broadcast or shared, and how a superpromoter exerts influence on others.

Enthusiasm

Take a look around you. Enthusiasm is to be found every-where and the average healthy and happy person will expe-rience the emotion of enthusiasm pretty much every day. Not necessarily about something big and important, as enthusiasm could equally be expressed about a movie, the weather, or about one's children and even a product you just bought. Psychologists will tell you that the ability to experience enthusiasm forms an important foundation for your happiness in life. If you are depressed it is impossible to experience any kind of enthusiasm, which explains why many depressed people experience their lives as being with-out purpose.[1] Thankfully, most of us are spared this fate, or only have fleeting encounters with that type of depression. Children, on the other hand, are usually brimming with enthusiasm, not all of it of the boisterous kind, either. To me it is quite touching to witness my three-year old son's enthusiasm, having come home with a bag of sweets from a birthday party at his nursery. As grown-ups we notice that the bag of sweets displays a somewhat rigid uniformity: the bag contains a box of raisins, a balloon and a biscuit. That, however, makes absolutely no difference to my son, or his friends; they always are equally happy every time they get a bag like that. A child's enthusiasm has a pure quality about it, unspoiled as yet by a social requirement to be seen doing something nice. They just really like to get that present, whether it seems little to us, or a lot. Alas, as we grow up it takes a lot more to make us really enthusiastic about something and keep feeling that way. The little everyday things are much less likely to make us enthusiastic, it takes something much more special to get us all fired up. Here follows a list of the most commonly given reasons for enthusiasm.

New & original

Mankind is forever in search of the stimulation of something new and exciting. If you encounter a new product, for example, it will always get more of your attention. And if you happen to like it, this may cause you to have an enthusiastic reaction that you would like to share with your friends and acquaintances. If they are indeed original, new products can very easily become a source of talk among people. On the other hand, just try and remember the last time you talked excitedly about an uninspired new product: having that boring label, "new & improved" just isn't the same as, "Wow, did you see that clever little thing!?"

Positive surprise

Enthusiasm will often be the result of having had a positive surprise. Take the average customer for example, who reacts positively to something new that is also truly original. However, receiving unexpected excellent service could equally be the surprise. The key is that in these instances their expectation level is being surpassed, a realization that carries the implication that a small step – but one that exceeds expectations – could result in the most positive surprise.

Authentic

The richer parts of the globe have been awash in advertising for so long now that we have developed a good deal of resistance to their messages. Not only do we lose the forest among the trees, we also learn to mistrust incoming commercial messages. In other words, with so much to choose from our attention gets scattered and the sincerity of the message is at best suspect. The same applies to brands. Those that are considered authentic and manage to avoid the appearance of money grubbing can count on an enthusiastic customer following. The ability to make people believe in your authentic passion[2] will be rewarded with enthusiastic clients and employees.

Promoting social contacts

Any services that are designed to smoothen or simplify communications with others will quickly receive an enthusiastic reception. As people we are quick to collectively adopt new and more efficient methods of communicating and to stay in touch. It blows the mind how email produced such a global change in our communications in just ten years. Similarly, the success of SMS, Twitter, Skype and the emergence of social networking websites such as Hyves, Facebook and MySpace is entirely due to the desire to keep in touch with others. The main engine for growth comes from people inviting others to start communicating with them in this manner. Clearly, if such a service meets an enthusiastic reception, its marketing is taken care of!

Practical, problem-solving, or perhaps just plain better
People tend to become enthusiastic about products that solve problems hitherto left unsolved, or sometimes even unaddressed. A good example would be the first beer crate with a handle in the middle, or the first time you use a navigation system or benefit from the ability to do 24/7 banking online. Problem-solving is great, but if a product or service is just better than someone else's, people can become quite enthusiastic about that as well. Most people like to deal with companies that happen to be the best in their area.

Open, transparent and honest
Customers in today's world demand from their companies that they maintain an open and transparent attitude. These new customers want to know whether any child labor was involved in the production of their purchase, whether the environment is being protected, and increasingly so today, what management is earning and paying in bonuses and if they are creaming too much off in profits. Modern technologies in combination with modern media have made the demand for transparency an unstoppable force. Politicians' expense claims are posted on the web, as are accounting scandals and various kinds of misinformation. The message behind these developments is clear: the best way in which to avoid disappointing your customers and to generate enthusiasm for you, your company and your products is by doing business openly, honestly and transparently. Another reason for this type of enthusiasm comes from the trend toward freedom of – previously protected – information.

Open source software, all of the wiki-type endeavors, the release of patents on a variety of medicines; these things, unthinkable only a short while ago, are now going mainstream. Any organization that dares to dismantle the protective wall surrounding its company secrets is certain to receive an enthusiastic response.

Beautiful and compelling

It is no secret that if you can strike a sensitive chord or create something compelling, enthusiasm usually will be the result. Certainly the advertising industry has been making use of this knowledge extensively. The vast majority of advertising makes use of beautiful or compelling images or music designed to evoke a certain type of emotion. But we can tug at the heartstrings in several ways. Then there is that old standby, humor, always a catchy way of getting people's attention.

And then there's cheap

Not all of us are destined to be the best, and perhaps it is also not possible to fulfill the other reasons for enthusiasm you've just been reading about. That leaves really only one other way of getting people to be enthusiastic about you, and that is to be the cheapest guy on the block. There are any numbers of examples of companies for whom this is a very successful strategy. These are the businesses that know where and how to find cheaper inputs – raw materials, labor or cheaper-faster-better processes to keep the competition at bay. However, it seems as if the incremental margins derived from efficiencies have been eroding.

Certainly, globalization has made it harder and harder to be the lowest cost competitor and yet remain profitable.

Low cost pricing is hard to sustain if the competition manages to drop its pricing to your level quickly. If the only thing that makes your customers enthusiastic about you is your low prices, they will not be loyal. The first lower price competitors will snatch them away from you. This kind of price war is elegantly described in their book *Blue Ocean Strategy*, by co-authors Kim & Mauborgne[3], who describe these cutthroat wars as a blood red ocean where many companies go under. The inescapable conclusion is that you must distinguish yourself in other ways as well; in other words, to chart a course to the deep blue ocean where demand is created rather than fought over.

Sharing enthusiasm

Have you ever noticed, when some girl or boy is telling some very enthusiastic story, how in no time they are surrounded by a crowd of other eagerly listening kids? We definitely become curious about somebody's enthusiasm about a pleasant experience. No doubt our curiosity is motivated by the desire to share in such an experience. The way superpromoters like to share with their environment things they have become enthusiastic about is represented schematically in figure 2.2.

Sharing your enthusiasm can be done in several different ways. One simple way it happens is when a person makes a recommendation to another.

"If I were you, I'd ask that ad agency to do the work"
"You really ought to try that new rinse"
"You know Bill, who works downstairs? He'd sort that out for you in no time"

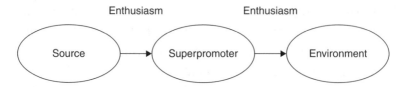

Figure 2.2 Superpromoter shares enthusiasm

One way or the other, the ad agency, hair rinses and Bill each produced enthusiasm among the people who are making the recommendations. Sharing enthusiasm can also be accomplished in less explicit ways, however. The following section will discuss the various ways in which enthusiasm may be shared around. There are three principal ways:

1. Spontaneous word-of-mouth
2. Passive word-of-mouth
3. Copy cat (herd) behavior

Spontaneous word-of-mouth
The first is a display of spontaneous behavior when people are so enthusiastic about something that they actively spread their enthusiasm around by word of mouth. Certain kinds of product are more eligible for this type of behavior than others. For example, cars, electronic gadgets or mobile phones are much more likely to be praised this way than the newest tax deferred savings instrument.

There are of course other factors that play a role in determining whether we will become spontaneous word-of-mouthers or not. Not all enthusiasts are ready, willing or able to share their enthusiasms around spontaneously. One factor would be whether we are a lone wolf, introverted type. Another factor affecting how quick we are to share our excitement is our degree of self-confidence. You have to be confident that your enthusiasm is going to be shared by others. It's no fun if your enthusiastic message gets no response, worse if it meets with scornful laughter. It's a bit like telling a joke that falls flat on its face. If your jokes don't make anybody laugh you'd soon stop telling them (some persistent jokers unfortunately fail to grasp this simple concept!). But if you get the crowd on your side you'll be telling more jokes like any stand-up comedian. The same thing applies to enthusiasm. If met with encouragement, that will make it easier for you to go on expressing your enthusiasms about whatever it is that got you going in the first place.

There is another reason to be careful with spontaneous acts of word of mouth. When you wax enthusiastic in recommending something to someone, there is always the risk that they will not have your positive experience. Telling someone to go to your favorite restaurant only to hear that they had an awful experience there can be very painful. Not to mention the blow to your reputation as a fine dining connoisseur. At some level, before giving out a recommendation, you make a conscious or subconscious calculation of the chances that the recipient will have a similar positive experience. It is much harder to give a spontaneous word-of-mouth approval about a restaurant that you know has a temperamental chef and erratic track record. The other thing you may try to factor in is the other person's known preferences. No steak houses for vegetarians or fish restaurants for the carnivores among your acquaintances. In other words, your assessment of the other's potential for enthusiasm is an important determinant of your spontaneous word-of-mouth behavior.

Finally, the size and shape of one's social network has a direct impact on how much enthusiasm can be shared around. The wider the network the wider one can spread one's enthusiasm; and so, fewer friends, lesser impact. Spontaneously made recommendations are most likely to occur among like-minded friends sharing similar interests. In Chapter 5, we shall be discussing more extensively the influence of a social network's structure.

Passive word-of-mouth

As the name suggests, passive word-of-mouth does not stem from the initiative of the enthusiast, it only happens when prompted. There are lots of reasons why word-of-mouth behavior is not always spontaneous. One obvious reason is that certain products and services are not often – or easily – part of the conversation. Our previous example of tax deferred savings instruments would be one; when was the last time you talked about these? But restaurants...we talk about them all the time! But if asked for an opinion or recommendation, most of us would unhesitatingly make a recommendation for a savings product we thought was good, assuming we know at least a little bit about it. The difference, therefore, between a spontaneous and passive word-of-mouth recommendation is that the former is offered unasked, while the latter needs someone to ask for it.

It is true that we also need some degree of self-confidence before delivering a word-of-mouth recommendation. Our approval does not necessarily lead to a happy outcome for all. Granted, there is some protection to be had from the fact you were asked in the first place; all you did was venture your opinion without actively forcing it on anyone. But to be confident that you know what you are talking about, your knowledge of the topic at hand is relevant. If you don't know the first thing about what you've been asked for, it will always be more reliable to say so and refer the person on to someone else, if you can.

It is of course possible to provide passive word-of-mouth recommendations without any particular type of enthusiasm. We've all been there before. None of the options seem particularly attractive, but since we were asked, we offer the least bad alternative. Don't expect enthusiasm, though! We would say that in such a case we can safely speak of word-of-mouth, or of a "recommendation", but that there is no superpromoting involved: no enthusiasm was being passed along with the recommendation.

Copycat/herd behavior

The least conscious manner in which enthusiasm can be transferred to others happens when it is passed along by copycat, or herd, behavior. The herd instinct is a powerful force in each of us. In essence, making a recommendation is an invitation to the other to be your copycat, to follow the herd. When making a recommendation, the invitation is explicit: you are telling the other to assume your behavior or attitude about something. By radiating your enthusiasm about – say – a product, your invitation is implicit. Herd behavior, which we are discussing here, as the third and final type of behavior, is by no means the least important. If anything it is the opposite. Herd behavior, being a copycat, the instinct to join the pack, is actually one of the most important determinants of human behavior.[4] Yet it does not feel tangible, since most of its activity takes place below the radar of our consciousness.

Mark Earls is a compelling advocate of the power of herd behavior. In his book, *Herd*, Earls offers us a convincing analysis of how human behavior can largely be explained by our instinct for copying the behavior of others. *Homo Sapiens* happens to be a social ape that starts to copy from the moment of birth. First, we begin by copying our parents and immediate family, later we include friends and other role models. Sometimes the notion that mankind is essentially made up of copying machines is difficult for those of us who have been raised with the Western ideal under which the highest goal we can achieve is individual freedom and individual creativity. That way of thinking can lead us to underestimate, and devalue, the value of herd behavior.

Mark Earls makes no secret of the fact that herd behavior is healthy. In fact, it is essential for functioning in any social environment or obtaining reliable information quickly. It would not be very efficient if we had to discover each and every thing by ourselves. The importance of copying behavior is demonstrated in people suffering from autism. Autistic people experience great difficulty with social behavior because of their lack of copying skills. They are unable to reflect the behavior of the person they are in contact with, which disrupts their social communication. The most successful people, on the other hand, tend to be excellent copycats. They can absorb useful information and socially desirable behavior in a flash, which of course propels them up the ladder of success with greater speed.

"How about creativity?", is likely to be the next question in response to this praise for the herd. The fact is that most creativity is nothing more or less than copycatting. Even the most original ideas will usually be based on some form of herd behavior, although the copycat aspect will be subtler, less obvious. Even the highly original Sir Isaac Newton admitted that if he had seen further it was by standing on the shoulders of Giants. Punks, Rasta's or Hiphoppers each wear a very distinctive dress code. Although their uniform is intended to distinguish them from the grey masses, this does not for a moment suggest their fashions are not based on herd instinct.[5] What this really means is that by combining different ideas from other groups or cultures we can be made to think something is highly original, while in fact it could just as easily be seen as a form of creative copying. In fact, as Newton would have confirmed, entirely new ideas are usually the result of an accident.

As mentioned earlier, most herd behavior takes place at a subconscious level. We all spend a good part of our day bouncing our self-image, like sonar, off that of our friends and colleagues. Even if a complete stranger sits down next to us on a park bench we're likely to start sitting in the same position. We cannot really control our urge to copy the behavior of others. In his engaging book, *Het Slimme Onbewuste* [The Smart Subconscious][6] Ap Dijsterhuis describes how people suffering from a certain kind of brain damage cannot control their copying behavior at all. These unfortunate people will compulsively copy the behavior of people in their environment; when for example sitting across the table from someone with their hands held a certain way; they feel compelled to do exactly the same. It would seem that your brains must be in good shape if you want to exercise some control over your herd instinct. Apparently, our need to copy is so strong that it takes more energy to control it than to just let it happen. This does not mean that we are all nothing more than uncontrolled copycats. We focus our copying behavior onto people that look like us, or that we would like to look like. We like to copy those whom we believe to have a greater store of brains, those who seem more self-confident, or happier. These descriptions, it turns out, fit the superpromoter quite well. Superpromoters use a product about which they are enthusiastic, this enthusiasm they radiate in a self-confident manner, and, perhaps without realizing it, in so doing exercise influence over their environment.

Influence

Much of what we have been discussing is really about influence. People are constantly influencing each other in a myriad of ways. Sometimes this happens consciously, when they are advising each other, or by talking with each other about any number of things. As we have seen, a large amount of influencing takes place at the subconscious level. That is what is goes on when we are following others: we take over their opinions and adopt their behavior. And as with all living creatures, this behavior is based on avoiding negative experiences while seeking out positive ones. We are likely to pay attention to a positive or negative recommendation from someone in our environment we consider to be reliable, just as we will copy the behavior of our peers or role models. The sincere enthusiasm of the superpromoter will exert influence on his social environment, but it will only have impact if his environment takes him seriously.

Robert Cialdini is a social psychologist who is considered to be an eminent scientist in the field of "influence". His book, *Influence: Science and Practice*[7], describes the six weapons of influence. Cialdini describes how you can use influencing to manipulate people into behaving in a certain way. His ideas appear to be largely derived from techniques employed by sales people. Now, the influence that our superpromoter has is based on real and sincere enthusiasm and not on some commercial bag of tricks. Nonetheless, there are elements from Cialdini's description that are equally relevant to the influence emanating from a superpromoter. Let us now take a look at the six weapons of behavioral influence, linking them to the superpromoter in each case.

Reciprocation

When somebody gives us something, we owe them; we are hardwired with the tendency to give them something in return. Cialdini provides us with a long train of research and cases confirming this observation. Reciprocity, the act of reciprocation, forms the cornerstone of our social structure while most of our norms and our value systems are directly attributable to this principle. This idea lies at the root of our thinking; popping up time and again in our figures of speech, for example, "one good turn deserves another", or, in the reverse, "an eye for an eye, a tooth for a tooth".

Reciprocation also plays an important role for the superpromoter, albeit of two different types. There is the reciprocation of someone's enthusiasm and then there is the other form by which a superpromoter exchanges enthusiasm to gain status and respect. If the superpromoter makes many valuable recommendations to his environment, he may reasonably expect his environment to return favors to him whenever chance permits. By that same logic, anyone with a good tip for a superpromoter is sure to give it to him. The tipster is building up credit with the superpromoter, which gives rise to the entirely reasonable expectation that the superpromoter will be offering a valuable recommendation back...and so on and so forth. Superpromoters will also tend to be quite open to advice coming from other superpromoters. Not only can they use it for their own purposes, but it also becomes currency to be used for influencing others. The exchange of ideas or advice forms a sound basis for a reciprocal relationship between superpromoters. If there is a trade gap, with the superpromoter "exporting" more recommendations that he "imports", the deficit will be transformed into incremental status and respect. A useful reward as it serves to increase his prestige and influence. Incidentally, when a superpromoter's recommendations are being taken up, this also means that his environment is providing confirmation of the validity of his recommendations.

Commitment & consistency

Human beings have an innate desire for consistency, which is why most of us tend to be loyal to our own opinions and behavioral patterns. Those people who seem to have consistent opinions and behavior are more likely to be taken seriously than others whose opinions change with the weather or whose behavior is inconsistent with their stated opinions. Once people have committed to a cause the expectation exists that they will remain committed. Accordingly, superpromoters will be more influential if they can demonstrate consistency and commitment.

The superpromoter's influence grows when he is able to offer a growing number of valued recommendations and appears to be consistent in the selection of brands or products he praises. Advice that backfires or a brand name that is praised one day and then damned the next will not be doing any good to the superpromoter's credibility. Of course a superpromoter is allowed to switch brands...but not too often. The logic is irrefutable: someone who switches too often is clearly making mistakes regularly and therefore not very reliable. And a superpromoter must come across as a most reliable figure.

Social proof

People have a strong tendency to do what others in their environment are doing; not only because it helps them to feel safe, but also because they are lazy. Generally speaking, most of us try to get away with putting as little effort as possible into thinking about the choices we have to make. Pondering each decision or choice would also be exhausting. Although we do end up making literally thousands of choices on a daily basis, most are made on autopilot. Most people come equipped with a kind of unconscious navigation system that tells them when to turn right or left. The software for this navigation system is built from a large number of comfortably worn-in patterns, in turn largely based on herd behavior. The herd instinct becomes very apparent when people are fearful or insecure. If a bomb were to explode in a busy marketplace, people would all end up running away, but following the same person. Or, using a less ominous example, if one person walking down the street starts looking up, right away there will be a few more scanning the skies and soon everyone will be trying to see what is going on...the herd instinct in action. But, as behavioral scientists will not fail to point out, following the herd is generally a sensible and safe choice, and it simplifies decision-making. It makes life much easier if you can just copy the behavior of those from whom you'd expect the "proper" behavior.

Superpromoters represent an important link in this chain of social herd behavior. They can be the real authority on the "proper" behavior to be followed, showing the rest of us what the right social norm is and what is trendy. It is because of their self-confidence, knowledge and social skills that they have the power to steer (no pun!) the herd in the right direction.

Liking

People are more easily persuaded by other people if they like them. Social scientists have been able to demonstrate that we tend to be more friendly to people who are attractive physically, and that we are likely to do them more favors. Tall men with deep voices are considered to be more attractive by both men and women. So it is no coincidence that such men have greater reproductive success in hunter-gatherer societies, or in modern ones tend to occupy more of the important functions than smaller and stouter types. The Napoleon-sized leader is more of an exception than rule, although his superpromoting skills are not in doubt!

Not only do we like physically attractive people, but also those who look like us, in more ways than just physically. A superpromoter's influence will have particular influence in an environment of similar people since he is more likely to be taken seriously in his own crowd. It is logical for people to search out birds of a feather to emulate. After all, they are being confronted with the same problems and opportunities as they are and that increases the probability that they have found good solutions for what is needed. Their flocks therefore tend to be made up of people of the same age, social class and attitudes.

Authority

There is no denying the increased influence of people who have been cloaked with formal authority. This applies to doctors or policemen, but also to the football trainer or chairperson of the neighborhood watch. The Milgram[8] experiments of the early sixties, testing people's willingness to deliver electric shocks to others, are an awful example of how far people can go if they are asked to do so by someone in authority. During the experiments a participant was given the role of "teacher" and instructed to administer electric shocks to another participant, the "learner" (victim), when he got the wrong answer to a question. The learners were actually actors and confidants of Milgram, but the real participants in the tests, the "teachers", were obviously not aware of this. Realistic sounding and escalating cries of pain notwithstanding, the greater portion of teachers (65%) continued administering the shocks right up to a potentially lethal dose of 450 volts. It is disturbing to know that we live among potential torturers, even more disturbing to consider that we might be one ourselves! When someone in an authoritative white lab coat tells us to do something we appear to be willing to go quite far to do as they wish.

Because superpromoters have been pre-selected based on their influence level, the percentage of people among them who already have a certain amount of authority is well above average. Superpromoters are therefore likely to have a certain degree of formal authority by virtue of the responsibilities they have assumed; or informal authority based on their expert knowledge on a given topic. Their authority could even be based on their charisma as a person. In business we'd call them the movers and shakers, the people who take the ultimate decisions, whether to do the deal, award the job or renew a contract. Movers and shakers don't have to be superpromoters, and superpromoters don't have to be movers and shakers. But if anybody combines the two, it makes for an extremely powerful combination. The influence they already have because of their responsibilities is turbocharged by their being a superpromoter to boot. That type of influence never stays within the confines of the superpromoter's company. Formal influence can be exercised by occupying additional functions elsewhere; as a non-executive director of another company or on the board of a charitable foundation. However, their informal exercise of influence may be many times more powerful. Given their status, superpromoters will often be approached for an opinion, or advice. When a mover and shaker displays enthusiasm about a potential supplier this fact alone can have great influence on commercial matters yet to unfold.

Scarcity
The perception of scarcity – or urgency – will allow people to be persuaded more easily. Used extensively in all forms of negotiation, it is one of the oldest selling tools around. By telling the doubters that your offer is "for a limited time only" or, "hurry, only two remaining!", you are using the sixth weapon of influence to reel them in.

When superpromoters are giving a recommendation, perceived scarcity or urgency will often play an important role. Their advice, unlike the broadcasting approach of advertising, will feel more like a hot tip...not shared with all and sundry. You sense that you've been handed an opportunity that cannot be ignored.

THE EXPONENTIAL POWER OF THE SUPERPROMOTER

Do not underestimate the degree of influence superpromoters have over others. Not only do they persuade others to buy certain products and not others, they also can advise their environment not to do business with the competition. And that is not all: part of a superpromoter's social environment will be made enthusiastic to such a degree that these people will become superpromoters themselves, turning more new people into potential superpromoters.

Sales growth could of course become exponential if this happens. Imagine that one superpromoter brings in five new customers, not overly impressive in its own right. But now let's suppose that this process repeats itself ten times, with each of the five new customers bringing in five new customers in turn. Give yourself a moment to estimate how many clients you'd have if this happens ten times. Then go figure it out on a calculator...

If you didn't happen to have a calculator at hand, the results are recorded below.

When one superpromoter brings in five new customers, who in turn bring in five more each, the number of new clients will be growing exponentially, as follows:

Step 1: 5 new customers
Step 2: 25 new customers
Step 3: 125 new customers
Step 4: 625 new customers
Step 5: 3125 new customers
Step 6: 15,625 new customers
Step 7: 78,125 new customers
Step 8: 390,625 new customers
Step 9: 1,953,125 new customers
Step 10: 9,765,625 new customers

In a perfect world, superpromoters could be responsible for bringing in almost 10 million new customers. There' s not much of a chance, unfortunately, of that happening in such a smooth progression. Not every superpromoter will deliver five new customers and not all new customers are superpromoters. Yet it is possible for one superpromoter to land much more than five new fish and some new products are so attractive that they are minting new superpromoters like nobody else. Google's exponential growth can be attributed to the way in which enthusiastic users infected others. Practically everybody heard about Google from other users. Pretty much everyone that I know has passed on the idea to try Google to friends. That is how Google became one of the most powerful enterprises on earth in just a few years. And it is not too hard to think of several other examples. The popularity of Alcopops, or the use of SMS messaging definitely exploded according to the exponential model we have just seen. The World Wide Web and (exponentially increasing) internet use have turned exponential growth figures into the realm of possibility for a great many companies.[9] Although it's impossible to calculate the speed at which people are influencing each other via email, forums and social media, we do know that many products unable to find their niche clientele in the world of bricks are now crossing the globe at the speed of clicks. This development only serves to strengthen the exponential powers of superpromoters. Lest we forget: negative news from disappointed customers travels and spreads just as quickly and is at least as powerful. We will return more fully to that issue in section "The Antipromoter: A Formidable Foe".

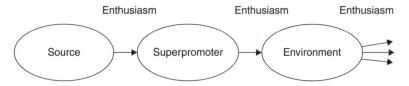

Figure 2.3 Transference of enthusiasm during exponential growth

When a product is sufficiently appealing the superpromoter will become enthusiastic, transferring this enthusiasm onto his environment, from where it spreads even further.

In his book, *The Tipping Point*[10], Malcolm Gladwell discusses how it happens that some behaviors, ideas, products or messages are adopted by masses of people, whereas others are not. These behavioral epidemics might, for example, be how people start buying a certain product in a big way, but it might also be voters' turnout resulting in an election upset, the escalation of violence in a hotspot, or a shift in perception such as happened to many after the Gulf War. Sometimes it can spread like a virus through social networks: a social epidemic. According to Gladwell it takes three kinds of people to cause the epidemic spread of behavior:

- **Mavens:** people who are the first to hear of new information.
- **Connectors:** people who operate in several different social networks and spread information from Mavens around in all of them.
- **Salesmen:** people who persuade others, acting within a specific social network.

When these three types of people are doing their job properly, they are responsible for a new movie becoming a box office hit, a book rocketing to the #1 spot on the list, or a politician being elected. Malcolm Gladwell develops his ideas and concepts in such a clear, entertaining and convincing manner that it is reasonable to expect that "tipping point" will inevitably become part of the language; the kind of expression that everybody uses. If in the landscape of ideas the amount of references being made to a certain theory is a meaningful measure, then Gladwell's "tipping point" measures up very nicely. *The Tipping Point* as well as other theories[11] discussing similar ideas helps to give us insight into how ideas and behaviors spread. The point being made in *The Superpromoter* is that the transfer of enthusiasm follows a similar path. There is a problem, however, in putting these ideas to practical use. The spread from Mavens to Connectors and from there to Salesmen and then on to the Masses represents behavioral complexity well beyond the scope of practical development. This is where the superpromoter is in a position to offer a solution.

For all practical purposes a superpromoter combines the role of Maven, Connector and Salesman. I can already hear voices of protest saying that's an oversimplification...and I'll be the first to agree. A tipping point is also a simplification; theories almost always are. But none of that changes the fact that it's difficult to put the tipping point theory into a pragmatic application. Superpromoters, on the other hand, since they feel involved with a product or company, are comparatively easy to find; they'll be happy to provide feedback and cooperate with you in word and deed. Simply put, with a superpromoter you can get to work on improving the odds that your product or idea spreads like an epidemic.

THE SUPERPROMOTER: COACH, MOTIVATOR AND INSPIRER

The energies of a superpromoter can have a two-way effect; his enthusiasm not only infects his environment, but it can also bounce back to the source. In fact, if the source is open to receive the enthusiasm in return, a superpromoter can perform the role of coach, motivator and inspirer. Although we're not always aware of it, this is basically happening around us all the time. In our daily life we're continuously going off to find our superpromoters. This is what happens every time a good friend offers you advice, gives you encouragement or opens your eyes for you: that's a superpromoter at work! After all, a good friend is supposed to be enthusiastic about you (would you call him a good friend otherwise?), and in sharing his enthusiasm with you, cross-infects you right back. This is what makes friendships so valuable: someone who appreciates you and is on your side. Good friends don't go saying unpleasant things behind your back, will warn you if others are doing so, and will be the ones who help you to grow as a person. We should not lose sight of the fact that people who have the best of intentions toward us are more numerous than we'd think; we might find them among customers or coworkers, for example.

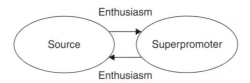

Figure 2.4 The superpromoter: Coach and motivator

The Superpromoter as coach

We need coaches to tell us how to do things better and how to beat the competition. Superpromoters can be possessed with both knowledge and willingness to be our coach. Customers, for example, are perfectly able to tell you what you should be doing better or what never to stop doing. They should be told whether you are receptive to this information, just as they should be aware that it is valuable for you to know what they are enthusiastic about. You, of course, will realize that you are talking to someone who is on your side when dealing with your superpromoter: here's a coach to cheer you on, yet be critical when needed.

There is no end of advantages to be gained from coworkers who are your superpromoters, and it's usually a big surprise to find out how much relevant knowledge they have. They can tell you things you didn't know about your own company, its markets, or even about yourself. Developmental feedback, you might call it, and colleagues who like you would certainly be happy to oblige you with their insights. Provided, of course, that you are willing to ask for the feedback. The experience is that coworkers who are quick to offer "spontaneous" criticisms are not usually the ones with your best interests at heart. Surely less so than your superpromoters. Colleagues who do care, on the other hand, are likely to offer constructive criticism only when they become really worried about something involving you. *Criticism* perhaps should be replaced with *advice*, because it is as important to receive negative as positive feedback. Regrettably, there are still not nearly enough professional occasions where it is usual to give spontaneous positive feedback. Superpromoters like to be the bringers of positive feedback, if asked. Survey the playing fields, and take note: there are plenty of coaches on the sidelines waiting for you to give them an opportunity to help. Well team, what are you waiting for!

The Superpromoter as motivator

Remember the description in the Introduction of what happens when a rock group transports their audience? As the fans are getting more and more fired up, they in turn are cheering on the group, who become even more carried away themselves. Quite powerful stuff, this positive feedback! In sports, it is fair to say, positive feedback is what makes beating your own record possible; with cheering fans to egg you on the unimaginable can happen.

I've had my own experience with the turbocharged energy produced by positive feedback. On January 4, 1997, I participated in a speed-skating marathon that passed through eleven Frisian towns, which the Dutch therefore call *De Elfstedentocht* (Tour of Eleven Towns). The 200 km course runs over frozen canals, rivers and lakes, and is often described as grueling. I had never skated more than some 50 km or so, and that had been some two years earlier. And this contest, which only happens when Holland has a serious cold spell, followed the over-indulgent festivities of the season...no way to get in shape! It couldn't have come at a worse moment, but since I had secured my starting place in a lottery I was determined to try. Together with my father, who is an experienced marathon skater, I faced the daunting odds: skating the equivalent of 4.75 marathons with freezing temperatures and harsh wind chill conditions, and very few daylight hours to help you see what you're doing. After 60 km I felt certain I would not make it to the halfway mark. Having started in the last group at 10 AM, it got dark quickly and the ice was in bad shape. The fact that I eventually made it to the finish line, with ten minutes to spare before the race was terminated at midnight, is largely due to the continuous positive feedback we received from the thousands of supporters cheering us on. Around every corner we were met with encouragement: "Keep going!", they were yelling; children were offering us fruit and the towns were filled with singing people. "You are going to make it!", we were told, again and again, as we were being supported on stretches of bad ice or staggered across the bare patches, "Don't give up!". Near the end, when we'd left the town of Dokkum, scrambling the last 25 km to the finishing line in Leeuwarden, I heard a group of girls shouting, "You guys are heroes!". Between my father and me there wasn't a dry eye to go around, and we staggered across the line after about 14 hours of the most arduous skating I'd ever dreamed of. But dreaming the impossible dream can become a reality with lots of positive feedback. Thanks, *Elfstedentocht*!

When companies, struggling to turn the corner or in need of help across rough patches, are being cheered on by their superpromoters, the people running the business will no doubt reach great heights of achievement. Their feedback builds self-confidence and charges the atmosphere with positive energy, as it fills everything you do with meaning....

The Superpromoter as inspirer

In addition to showing you how to improve some things, superpromoters can also inspire you with entirely new and creative thoughts. Of course that is less likely to happen if you are looking for specific improvements: when asking a superpromoter for suggestions on what to improve, they are likely to stay inside the thinking-box of what is already there. Useful, of course, but you'd not be realizing their full potential. You can tap into it when you get them to start thinking about things that don't exist yet. The strength of a superpromoter stems from their ability to conceive of new products and services or even to dream up entirely new markets. The ability to do so comes from the ability of superpromoters to see needs from the perspective of customers. His needs and those of his environment are blended into one, which makes the superpromoter ideal for new product development. Not merely enthusiastic and a team-thinker, superpromoters have an ability to sniff out potentially great innovations. Through their ongoing conversation with many people, something they love to have, they are continually engaged in their own market research. Any positive reaction to their enthusiasm from their contacts can tell them if something has potential. This is what superpromoters seem to live for, a fruitful chat and recognition from their environment!

One of the things that make superpromoters into such effective developers of new potential is their unencumbered approach to any given issue. Theirs is not the restricted or preordained route that sees only that a possible/impossible type scenario can exist for companies. Their way opens up all kinds of new angles, ideas or opportunities. It is very easy to see how it works on the web. Those companies that are willing to experiment with forms of crowdsourcing and co-creation are demonstrating their ability to achieve wonderful results.[12] Co-creation specifically refers to several forms of interactive collaboration among organizations and individuals and among individuals themselves. The new generation of web technology – usually referred to as Web 2.0 – has made it much easier for people to interact with each other, which has accordingly provoked the creation of innovative forms of collaboration between consumers and businesses. LEGO Mindstorms'[13] project is a wonderful example of how LEGO in co-creation with customers has led to successful new-product development. Customers are being encouraged to re-design LEGO products or even to develop new ones. If LEGO considers one of these designs to have potential, they'll take it into production, sharing profits with creators. This makes it possible for new ideas to germinate with amateurs, not a professional design department. Several highly successful new ideas have been developed this way already, giving LEGO the opportunity to be more innovative, at less expense. As a bonus, LEGO fans become more and more enthusiastic about Mindstorms and find more and more to talk about.

Web-based technology is not what makes a superpromoter join in co-creation with a company, but it simplifies the effort considerably. For successful co-creation, both enthusiasm and information must be shared. Superpromoters can keep a co-creation project alive with their enthusiasm, and it will benefit from their involvement right from the start. That type of involvement will be a source of motivation for the superpromoter to spread the word when a new product comes to market. You might say: "If we build it for you, you might come. If we build it with you, you are already there."[14]

Superpromoters don't necessarily need to get paid for their efforts; being appreciated goes a long way. They like to participate in developing new products, or perhaps in managing a business or process. Online co-creation represents one way of going about this but it is equally possible to have minds meet at some old-fashioned get-together round a table. Superpromoters can be an encouraging source of inspiration during such sessions.

Consumer based new-product development is not the only area where superpromoters can be a source of inspiration. The superpromoter can be the bringer of innovative ideas in the service industry with similar ease. If you give a superpromoter an opportunity to contribute, all kinds of ideas start emerging from the deep. Usually these contributions remain submerged if the objective is limited to making modest improvements. Hidden processes come to light that can have an enormous impact on sales, and equally on the company's reputation.

> While talking to a superpromoter of the Dutch airline, KLM, it became clear that his enthusiasm was based on an experience of several years before. He told the story of how he had become a KLM superpromoter more than ten years ago because the flight attendant had most pleasantly surprised him. What happened? He was on his way to make a twelve-month honeymoon trip around the world with his new wife. But, since they wouldn't be coming back home for a while, they had asked the flight attendant if she might be able to take their thank-you notes back with her in order to mail them back in Holland. Unfortunately, security regulations did not permit the flight attendant to accept any packages from a passenger. Our budding superpromoter and his bride were somewhat disappointed, of course, although they did have some understanding for the flight attendant's problem. A little while later the flight attendant returned, telling the couple

that she had been able to arrange something nice in return for not being allowed to help. She expressed her wish that this might compensate the newlyweds for their disappointment. The flight attendant had arranged an upgrade for the couple to First Class for the remainder of the long flight. When they got to their first class seats there were two glasses of champagne and some hors d'oeuvres waiting for them. The gesture touched the newlyweds profoundly. Our KLM superpromoter told of his sincere appreciation for the gesture, and that since that time he had always made a point of flying KLM whenever possible. And he has been telling this story for the last ten years to whoever would listen. During those ten years he estimates telling his tale more than a hundred times. It is a nice story, clearly, and a huge compliment for the flight attendant who had understood so well what being client oriented means. But there is more to it than that. These kinds of events have an enormous influence on a company's image. Imagine for a moment that our friendly flight attendant had had this kind of effect on one hundred passengers, turning them all into superpromoters. Then imagine that the flight attendant had 99 colleagues who were equally client focused. If so, these flight attendants would cause 10,000 superpromoters to be born, who, cumulatively, would then tell 1,000,000 friends, family and acquaintances enthusiastically about their great KLM experience! No advertising campaign could outperform that type of word-of-mouth energy, which has the additional benefit of not costing KLM anything extra!

Now, KLM is obviously a customer-oriented enterprise; airlines must take service very seriously. Having made that statement, it would seem that they nonetheless out-did themselves with the honeymooners; this is more than could be expected of just friendly staff. But precisely these kinds of spontaneous acts may lead to long-term enthusiasm from their customers. Clearly, these types of act are hard to orchestrate and manage. The most important contribution KLM can make toward achieving that goal is to hire the right kind of flight attendants who have a talent for dealing with such situations. The implication is that KLM must ensure that their training does not seek to prevent flight attendants too much from doing what they might wish to do, or create manuals with overly strict rules. The flight attendants must be given the freedom to act spontaneously, and that behavior should be rewarded with positive reinforcement. It is highly probable that the flight attendant in our story was never given any form of feedback for her customer-oriented act; who knows, perhaps her supervisor, on hearing of the incident, would have reprimanded her for favoring some passengers over others. Not that her supervisor would be to blame for the fact that their own training did not prepare them for these situations; yet, it is unlikely that the supervisor would be conscious of the positive effect the flight attendant's act has on the image of KLM, working its magic through the subsequent enthusiastic behavior of the superpromoter.

If the flight attendant, and her colleagues of course, were to receive positive feedback in these cases from supervisors, or, possibly even more importantly, from the superpromoters themselves, there is no doubt that it would encourage more client-focused behavior by the flight attendants. The cabin crew would also discover what works and what doesn't, and which passengers are most susceptible to these attentions. Giving the flight attendant more scope for doing something nice for their passengers would also improve their job satisfaction, not to mention the satisfaction of having people appreciate what they do. In that type of working environment the most customer-oriented flight attendants would be likely to remain with KLM for longer, developing a critical mass of positive acts. If all of these things were to happen, there would be a growing body of superpromoters telling their social networks about their positive experiences with KLM.

The airline industry has of course been measuring customer satisfaction and loyalty for decades, on the whole returning similar results every time. People are reasonably satisfied, with some complaining about legroom or a disappointing meal. There are a few who have had a genuinely unpleasant experience, usually involving ticketing problems or lost or delayed luggage. But, this type of customer-satisfaction research does not unearth the superpromoter who has been screaming how wonderful KLM is at the top of his lungs. That is because the research is looking for things to improve, not for superpromoters. In fact, enthusiastic customers are not given much of a platform from which to broadcast their feelings; something we know superpromoters just love to do! Furthermore, superpromoters are often enthusiastic about subjects the company does not even know about, which means that by making the effort to find out about what you're doing well, you probably can get some bright new ideas. Provided you invite your superpromoters to participate.

THE ANTIPROMOTER: A FORMIDABLE FOE

Should a superpromoter be viewed as friend or foe? From a business perspective, is he an opportunity or a threat?

Unfortunately, there is no simple answer. Superpromoters can be either a friend or an enemy, but never both at the same time. He will be either one or the other. Like Longfellow's little girl, when they are good they are very, very good, but when they are bad they are horrid. It is unlikely that you will ever encounter a neutral superpromoter; they'd be far too involved with your brand or product to be capable of neutrality. When people have become enthusiastic about something their expectation level will remain fairly high, although it is safe to say that a company will have some leeway with its superpromoters. They are not about to abandon ship at the first sign of failure. Rather, like loyal football fans, they will go to great lengths to defend you. Yet even diehard fans would expect the coach to be sent packing if the club cannot end a losing streak. Superpromoters will be following matters attentively and speak up if something doesn't meet with their approval. This is also the time when a superpromoter will expect something to be done about his criticism. If the company does not heed these comments, or even moves in an opposite direction, there is always the risk that the superpromoter will stop being your loyal friend. That is how an antipromoter is born: your most formidable foe.

Coca-Cola found this out to its detriment when they introduced New Coke in 1985.[15] The beverage giant was not only going to introduce a new soft drink to its markets it was also going to discontinue their traditional and familiar soda pop. All of a sudden Coca-Cola was no longer available. This rash act almost destroyed the company. Diehard Coca-Cola fans were outraged at having their favorite soft drink taken away from them. The reaction grew into a spontaneous revolution, with New Coke being boycotted on a massive scale. To its credit, the Coca-Cola Company changed tactics fairly promptly and brought their iconic "Classic" Coke back in a hurry. Having learned a profound lesson then, the company will now go to great lengths to preserve the authentic character of their brand. When they eventually introduced their new plastic bottles, the company made sure they had the same familiar shape as the original glass ones. Coca-Cola is again one of the strongest brands, and its superpromoters guard the brand's authenticity as fiercely as the company protects its secret Coca-Cola recipe. A fine example of what happens when a company changes in ways disapproved of by their superpromoters: Enter the dark alter ego...the antipromoter.

By definition a superpromoter who turns against you becomes an antipromoter, who can be defined as follows:

The antipromoter is decidedly negative, shares this negativity with others and thereby influences his social environment.

Accordingly, antipromoters will demonstrate the following three characteristics:

1. An antipromoter is pronouncedly negative
2. An antipromoter shares this negativity with others
3. An antipromoter has influence

Antipromoters are not quite the same as a dissatisfied customer. For one reason or another they have been disappointed, have turned decidedly against a company and will actively advise people to refrain from doing business with their target. As you can see, the antipromoter is active and very much involved. They could be former superpromoters who have turned sour, but could also be someone who, potentially, might have been a superpromoter, but for whatever reason developed a negative attitude instead. It is also a common occurrence for one brand's superpromoter to be another brand's antipromoter. This is the result of a conscious choice, and therefore something to be taken seriously.

As the Coca-Cola case has suggested, antipromoters should not be considered indifferent toward you or your brand or product. It may be possible in some cases to recapture the loyalty and enthusiasm of the superpromoter, if the source of their frustration is removed and amends are made. In doing so, the antipromoter is likely to feel appreciated and could conceivably be returned to the fold as a superpromoter. Most of us will recognize that when our complaint has been dealt with politely, respectfully and satisfactorily, our negative feelings are suddenly transformed into positive ones. Only when matters are dealt with swiftly does an about-turn like this have a chance of happening. If there is no prompt remedial action from the offending company, chances are that a superpromoter will have already forged strong ties with another brand, making it harder to reconcile. Consider the social implications of telling everyone not to do business with a company: their renewed love affair would at least raise eyebrows and more likely affect their credibility as superpromoters.

It is also possible that someone became an antipromoter because they had an unpleasant initial encounter, heard something bad about the company or received a negative recommendation. If the company can discover how this happened it might be possible to rebuild confidence; re-converting the antipromoter to superpromoter once again. In a situation such as this the antipromoter is likely to be receptive toward getting some additional attention, which then provides the opening for repairing the relationship. Here is the story of a superpromoter of a well-known fashion label. She was very disappointed when the zipper broke on a coat she'd bought only five weeks earlier, and so she tried to exchange it at the shop where she had bought it. Their immediate reaction was a flat refusal, using the lame excuse that "the guarantee" had expired. Then, plumbing new depths, the sales assistant even tried to insinuate that the coat had been carelessly treated. Unsurprisingly, the superpromoter became really furious and transformed into an antipromoter on the spot: not only of the sales assistant, the shop, but also of the label. She vowed never to buy anything from that shop again and to send the strongest complaint possible to the clothing brand's website.

Her complaint got an immediate response from the company. They sent her a new coat, with a personal letter apologizing profusely for the inconvenience as well as for the uncooperative attitude displayed by the retailer. She appreciated the gesture enormously. Although she has remained an antipromoter of the shop, her relationship with the clothing brand has actually improved. Having received such a satisfactory response to her complaint fired up her level of enthusiasm; most of her friends have been told of her happy experience by now. If, on the other hand, the brand had not responded or had only offered an inadequate response, she would have shared her bad experience with those same people as well. It would be quite a story: the poorly made coat that got ruined when the zipper came apart, the awful service in the shop and then the indifferent reaction from the brand label, would have been more than enough to turn her into a dedicated antipromoter. An antipromoter who would put a lot of effort into warning her social network not to buy those awful clothes and to avoid shopping in that store or buy that brand.

We should not underestimate the power of this type of negative messaging. Market research indicates that negative consumer advocacy has greater power than positive advocacy. Research performed by the London School of Economics,[16] for example, shows that among companies they have analyzed, a 1% growth of positive consumer advocacy equals turnover growth £ 8.8 million, whereas a 1% increase in negative consumer advocacy can be correlated to a decline in turnover equal £ 24,8 million. Most people are very sensitive to negative advocacy of products or services; nobody wants to buy the proverbial pig in a poke. It is much easier to scare someone off from buying a lemon than to get them enthusiastic about purchasing something. The suggestion *not* to buy also carries a lower risk of damaging one's reputation. Keeping someone from making a good acquisition with negative advocacy will in most cases be less painful than if they'd make a bad acquisition based on your "sound" advice. When you are being told not to eat in such-and-such restaurant, you'll never know whether you might have had a decent meal there. And if later you discover that it turns out to be a good place to eat after all, you can always still go there. But, having a bad experience in a restaurant that was recommended to you can ruin your entire evening. A negative experience is likely to be of greater weight and will diminish your confidence in the abilities of the source of your information. Not someone you'll be asking for a recommendation again any time soon...

Since people are more susceptible to negative messages, the antipromoter's job is made easier. The ease of spreading messages extends into other media channels. Journalists also prefer to write about bad news – it grabs their readers more quickly, who naturally prefer to be reading those things. The superpromoter's alter ego certainly looms as a credible threat to any organization. But there is one bright spot. Antipromoters do have one positive characteristic: because they are active communicators, it is quite easy for you to find out about them and their message. You'd probably have noticed them the first time when they were still your superpromoter. Unfortunately, when they were not heard and taken seriously, they turned into a dreaded antipromoter. So, keep it in mind; before they turn into antipromoters, the superpromoter will let you know of their disappointment. There is a far greater likelihood that a superpromoter will lodge a complaint with a business than the average customer. First, their emotional involvement is stronger, and second, superpromoters tend to be more assertive; that is how they became influential within their social networks to begin with! There is a natural assumption on the part of superpromoters that people listen to them, and therefore the odds are that they will equally make sure they're heard with a negative message. Looking at it from this perspective, it might be productive to think of their (constructive) criticism as a gift. And if the criticism is properly handled it will encourage the superpromoter and only serve to increase his enthusiasm. In conclusion: the best remedy against the rise of the antipromoter is to listen well and act accordingly.

There are times when a lost cause is a lost cause. If the antipromoter has been disillusioned to the extent that you cannot get through to them anymore, it is probably wise to leave matters alone. Antipromoters who, for example, spend their time online tearing down a business are very likely a lost cause from the company's point of view. Worse, when businesses do respond to the onslaught aimed at them, their reaction will probably act like a red rag to a bull. In these circumstances a superior strategy is to have your superpromoters enter the arena against combative antipromoters. The superpromoters are naturally inclined to rise in your defense in any case, but a helping hand with supporting information, or, say, technical support could make the difference in the confrontation. One way is to offer superpromoters a platform, a topic we will return to in a little while. All is not lost! With a fighting force of super-promoters among your ranks you're well protected from the antipromoters' forces.

Now that we have got to know the superpromoter and antipromoter a little better, it is time for us to see what different types of superpromoters there are. This will be the subject of the remainder of the current chapter. However, it is a reasonable assumption that for each category of superpromoter we will be discussing there also exists a corresponding antipromoter category. Yet, we will not be offering equal time to antipromoters during every step of our discussion of superpromoters; not only because *The Superpromoter* would be less readable... but also because the emergence of antipromoters can easily be avoided if only you pay close attention to your superpromoters!

WHAT KIND OF PEOPLE ARE SUPERPROMOTERS?

Is a superpromoter a particular type of human being? Or do they come in different shapes and sizes for different situations, for example, for specific brands or products? In fact, both are true. Certainly some people are born with superpromoting characteristics; these are the people who become enthusiastic more often, feel the urge to share their enthusiasms more keenly and have above average influence in social groupings. Then there is the other kind: the super-promoter whose enthusiasm and influence extends only to a particular product, or only to specific circumstances. That could be the computer geek whose influence is limited to IT stuff, or the music teacher whose opinion only counts when buying a musical instrument. Superpromoters can represent a specific customer group and also themselves, as individuals. Therefore, and depending why you need them, you can determine which type to zoom in on. This section discusses superpromoters in general. In the next section we'll be meeting the situational superpromoter.

All of us will have come across a chronic superpromoter, or two. Just run through your social networks for a moment and you'll be able to identify a few. Recognizable by their exuberant enthusiasm and ability to infect others with their excitement, their friends and acquaintances would no doubt use exactly these typical character traits to describe a superpromoter's personality. Research suggests that approx-imately 20% of people match these personality traits. Here are some of the most typical characteristics displayed by superpromoters.

Optimistic, enthusiastic and curious

As natural optimists, superpromoters find much to be enthusiastic about. They tend to have more favorite brands than the average consumer and it is important to them to share their enthusiasms for brands and products with others. Superpromoters have lots of ideas and are endowed with a colorful imagination. This makes them the right candidates to join in your brainstorming sessions. Because superpromoters are curious about new products they are quite open to advertisements as well as other types of corporate communication. If a new product hits the shelves that gets superpromoters excited, it offers them a perfect opportunity to surprise their social networks with something new. They are, in short, always on the lookout for new information; a web surfer, newsletter subscriber and consumer of advertising messages...the superpromoter's radar is always on. The energy spent on this is fueled not only by curiosity, which is in their nature, but also by the sincere desire to be the most informative person for you to talk to.

Critical consumer

Our superpromoter isn't only enthusiastic, quite the contrary; in fact, they can be highly critical. Part of the reason for this lies in their need to maintain their reputation. If a business they recommend doesn't live up to expectations, their reputation is affected as well. It seems that superpromoters only become enthusiastic when they are convinced that a product or brand truly deserves it. They must be careful about how they wield their influence: if they use it unwisely in their social groups they may lose their authority. Their best defense is to be well-informed at all times, which means cross-checking information from several sources whenever possible. These are people who read professional literature and scour company websites for information. Superpromoters are frequent visitors of forums and blogs, leaving a trail of messages behind. As noted earlier, superpromoters make clear decisions and tend to be simultaneous antipromoters of competing brands. Just as they are outspoken about what they like, superpromoters will speak their mind about what they do not like. They'll be as explicit about brands they like as about the ones they discourage their friends from using.

Social being

Superpromoters, to a far greater degree than the average consumer, are social beings. They are at their happiest in the company of others: their social identity is their life. They allow themselves to be influenced by their environment, just as they can exercise significant influence on others. Their interest in people and their opinions is above average; accordingly, their social calendar is much busier, with friends, the people in their club or professional association, or with colleagues outside office hours. Their Rolodexes and the address book in their mobile phones are always filled and up-to-date. Networking takes organization! Because they are continuously interacting with other people, the superpromoter can easily become enthusiastic about new things picked up from others. They don't always have to be the one who discovers a new product, for example. They are genuinely interested in a wide variety of topics, which in any event provide them with further information to use for the purpose of spreading some surprising news in their group. Or beyond, as superpromoters will happily absorb information coming out of their group and broadcast it to the outside world. Superpromoters have been quick to grasp the advantage of doing their social networking online; they spend above average time there, whether professionally or privately. They are more often members of social network sites, registering more online friends than average as well.

It is through their social identity that superpromoters distinguish themselves from "regular enthusiasts". The things they have to say are normally tailored for their environment. This became readily apparent from market research we conducted not that long ago. Blauw Research, working on behalf of the Dutch Railways, recently made an evaluation of a trial rail ticket for retired people. Many customers were decidedly enthusiastic about the advantages of the new ticket, yet the interesting discovery was that typical comments from superpromoters among the test group always included the social aspect.

> *"Everybody I know is envious of my new ticket. I'm convinced most of my friends also want one."*
> *"During my trip several people asked me what kind of ticket I had. They were very enthusiastic."*
> *"I have been telling everyone I know about this new ticket. People seem surprised and very interested."*

This is a selection of spontaneous comments from superpromoters appearing at the end of the questionnaire. Stressing the social interactions that have resulted from their special rail ticket, it provides us with a clear indication of how super-promoters articulate their social identity. If they are being given the freedom to speak, they will address the world coming from the viewpoint of their social environment. On the other hand, any spontaneous comments made by other enthusiastic customers were strictly limited to their own personal sense of enthusiasm. From this category of people you'd expect to receive answers along the lines of, "I think it's great that I can travel much more using this ticket." Their social environment, however, was never part of their frame of reference. All in all, it offered us a practical and powerful example of the demonstrable differences between the average enthusiasts and those of superpromoter caliber.

Influential advisor

Usually the superpromoter will be the touchpoint of a group; they like to help others by giving advice in various forms. And they will not be shy about confronting others with their – possibly contrary – opinions. They are asked for advice or an opinion more often than others, and their pronouncements will usually be listened to attentively. Superpromoters do not always need to get up on their soap-boxes to address the world; instead, people come to them seeking their views. Convincing in debate, they are not easily bested in a discussion: the superpromoter is to be taken seriously. Because they exert demonstrable influence over their environment, their judgments or preferences are often copied. One of the ways this copying behavior manifests itself is when people in their network are seen to be using the brands and products recommended by the superprom-oter in their group. It's happening all the time.

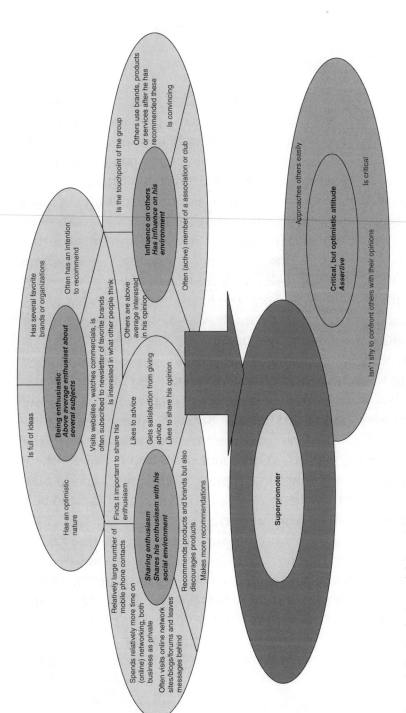

Figure 2.5 Analysismodel Superpromoter

THE SITUATIONAL SUPERPROMOTER

The previous section looked at what kind of people super-promoters tend to be. Not all superpromoters fall into a standardized "typecast"; many only become one for a specific product or category of products, or perhaps only in a specific type of situation. This type of situational super-promoter is not necessarily a natural-born leader of their group, or at least not in every situation. Some can even be rather shy and introverted. It is in a specific area that they blossom and can exert their authority. Consider for a moment and you will recognize exactly the type of people I mean. Perhaps at work, the ones always somewhat in the background reveals themselves as passionate cooks in the kitchen. Suddenly, you begin to notice them as they talk about what goes on in their kitchen; someone who knows his wine, herbs and spices, and what works in a kitchen and what doesn't. They are the ones telling friends, or the local cookery club what kind of equipment to buy. This enthusiast displays a marked preference for particular brands of cookware, tells others all about them and persuades them to go out and buy those brands. Companies that are marketing their kitchenware would find this enthusiast to be a most valuable superpromoter.

And then there's another superpromoter, a classic car nut who is quite passionate about one well-known make of car, but also about his insurance company because they allow him to insure his cars at reasonable rates. Not easy to find, apparently. The online classic car community of which he is a member has posted his praise for the car insurance, and several other members have since taken out the same policy. Unlikely to recommend anything to anybody in the other aspects of his life, our classic car insurance superpromoter has been selling insurance policies tailored for other classic car fans. The likely result is that in the classic car community more people will become enthusiastic about this product, and it will spread like wildfire. This would be valuable, for owners of classic cars, but certainly also for the insurer! It is a safe assumption that for every brand or product there will be clusters of superpromoters who do not readily fit the superpromoter-personality stereotype.

How to harness the energies of a situational Superpromoter

By now it should be clear that situational superpromoters could be of incalculable value to a business. Let us take a look at an example of how a business or marketing manager should be looking at these opportunities. Suppose that Heineken Beer decides to launch a new beverage to be consumed at barbecues. That's the perfect time for Heineken to consult with the superpromoters. The first question would be: who are they...exactly? In this case it would make sense to look for barbecue fans that happen also to be Heineken superpromoters. It should not prove too difficult to find some people with these two attributes. Having assembled your brainstorming team, you then pour out all of the ideas you've had for the design and ingredients of your new drink. Every time we do this at Blauw Research, we are surprised at how well these groups are able to fuel your creative thinking. Taking another example, let's consider the case of the civil servant responsible for deciding where to install new parking meters in a hardworking industrial city, Rotterdam, for example. It would no doubt be a tough job to find superpromoters for parking meters, but it would make sense to have Rotterdam's superpromoters participate in deciding where to place the meters. If they were supportive of the proposed layout, it would make the job of selling the parking meters to the people of Rotterdam much easier. As these examples suggest, how you can best harness the energies of situational superpromoters depends on the specific situation. In fact, this exercise can force you to consider carefully which groups of enthusiasts are important to you and your business. From both perspectives: which superpromoters are likely to become enthusiastic about your new product, and which enthusiasts will turn against you if you're not careful. If you have surveyed your landscape well, these groups can then be invited into your decision-making process.

THE SUPERPROMOTER APPEARS IN DIFFERENT GUISES

In *The Superpromoter* we are mostly after our quarry in their role as a consumer. The following chapter will discuss at length the role of superpromoters in the development of our understanding of customer orientation. This section will take a brief look at a number of other roles, although each would be worthy of more extensive treatment in other circumstances.

The Superpromoter as colleague

Among your colleagues you could probably find a number of superpromoters. Every business, every organization, will include a group of colleagues who are enthusiasts and exercise a greater degree of influence than others. These are the men and women who at social gatherings proudly tell people about the company they work for. They also have a significant influence on the atmosphere at work, and are key internal communicators on the informal company circuit. Involved and positive, they are loyal to their company, yet not without the ability to be critical where needed. Constructive criticism is a key feature among superpromoters. This is logical; since they want their company to do well, and they are always ready to participate in whatever is needed to improve things. Whenever research is conducted on employee satisfaction, the feedback from superpromoters is markedly different from that received from an average group of employees. And because people working for the company are enthusiastic, it reduces the likelihood that a company's senior management will assume a defensive posture against it employees during times of stress. Because employees have shown that they care, senior management in turn will offer a greater degree of support to their employees. And since this group, like founders of a company, share a belief in its mission, they are the ones you'd want to listen to and keep. That coin's flipside is that the superpromoting colleague can turn into a fearsome enemy if not heeded.

As we saw earlier, the superpromoter turned antipromoter will be sounding off about everything: company strategy, management, products, other people in the company and so on. This negative messaging is not restricted to within the walls of the company; the outside world, even clients, and anybody else the antipromoter can reach will hear it. Most of us consider complaining to your customer about your company to be pretty desperate, yet antipromoters have no qualms about telling them how they would love to help but are not allowed to by their company. By registering their disapproval in this manner, the antipromoter is placing himself "outside" the company. Customers usually do not care for such explicitly disloyal behavior, but will also be unimpressed by more implicit signs: the antipromoter's loss of client focus and lack of customary enthusiasm for their job. Antipromoters are bad for you, your company and its reputation, your customer relationships and the atmosphere at work. Superpromoters on the other hand are a company's most loyal and trustworthy employees.

The Superpromoter as citizen

Our investigation into superpromoters in all of their guises has also shed some light on their role as civic-minded members of the public. People who are dissatisfied about something usually dominate the involvement of the public in civic matters. The media, who are always happy to shine a spotlight on complainers, supports and in fact encourages negative reporting. The enthusiastic citizen is not often heard in public. This group is less likely to seek attention from government or media because they don't need to. Personally, they're doing just fine. But in answer to the call to participate they arrive in enthusiastic numbers. In this regard superpromoters respond very differently from dissatisfied citizens or special interest groups. There is also a certain democratic balancing logic to be found in lending your ear to superpromoters as well as to the complaining citizen. Listening only to special interests or complaints inevitably leads to an undemocratic result; superpromoters play an important role in everyday life and have an equal right to be heard! In listening to them, one also hears the group, or groups, they represent, as superpromoters are the influential mouthpieces within their social context.

Furthermore, engaging with superpromoters allows you more ready access through them to their social groups, which otherwise might be inaccessible. Think of the superpromoters representing ethnic minorities for example: they are exactly the right people to tell you what is going on in their backyard, but also to help you propose and deliver possible solutions back to their group. Research indicates that superpromoters within ethnic groups tend to be younger, better educated and more fluent in the host language. They are much better placed to tell us how the first generation of immigrants (usually their parents) feels about specific societal issues than that generation can do on its own. These superpromoters can be an ideal sounding board for a government trying to communicate with ethnic communities.

With regard to superpromoters of governmental initiatives, it is usually best not to attempt to define them in terms of their enthusiasm but to use their level of involvement as your measure instead. We were requested by the Dutch Ministry of the Interior and Kingdom Relations (Home Affairs) to attempt a definition of superpromoters for a government program called *"Safety in Public Work"*.

It would be hard to imagine defining any member of the general public as an "enthusiast", or even to feel closely

> The *Safety in Public Work* program seeks to ensure that employers and employees working for the public can perform their task in a safe and respectful environment. Specifically this means that employees doing public work are expected to treat members of the public with respect and understanding, and are entitled to expect the same in return. If a situation arises that requires the actual repression of violence and aggression, then government, employer and employee will each have circumscribed responsibilities. If such responsibilities cannot be met for whatever reason, the *Safety in Public Work* team are there to support and assist employers and employees.

involved with this topic; it is too unpleasant for that. So, in this case we used the superpromoter definition as follows:

1. The superpromoter is involved
2. The superpromoter shares their opinion
3. The superpromoter has influence

However, it soon became obvious that many of the program's supporters in fact can be classified as superpromoters. These were all regular citizens of which the Ministry up to that moment barely had any inkling. There even existed superpromoters who maintained a special site on the popular Dutch Social Networking site, Hyves that had attracted thousands of members. These superpromoters would feel honored if they were invited by the Ministry to help develop their policy program. The mere fact that they bothered to organize their sites and managed to recruit thousands is most interesting.

The Superpromoter as opinion leader

Wikipedia defines an opinion leader as someone who is held in high esteem by those that accept his or her opinions. That can be at the individual, but also at the societal level. The opinion leader is an agent who is an active (mass) media user, and uses it as a tool for spreading his opinions and/or to fuel a debate on – say – actual public issues. In many cases the superpromoter is not an opinion leader in the more formal sense of the term, but just a regular enthusiastic man or woman who happens to be sharing his opinions and thereby influencing others. It is not difficult to imagine how powerful the combination of being a superpromoter and an opinion leader is. For example, a journalist expressing practically unbridled enthusiasm for a new play could influence theatre attendance dramatically with his rave review. Or in the reverse, causing a play to flop because he panned it. We see superpromoters being put to work in politics to influence elections: politicians in every country have their own Oprah Winfreys superpromoting their own Barack Obamas. It should not be a great surprise to us how much influence an enthusiastic opinion leader can have. After all, by definition they have both influence and the ability to reach a large number of people. It is probably a fair statement that this activity is as old as mankind. Nonetheless, the winds of change have been blowing with increasing force in recent times.

Before the arrival of the World Wide Web and true "mass" media it was much easier for opinion leaders to influence public opinion. This may sound contradictory, since it has become so much easier to reach a large mass of people. However, capturing their attention in a meaningful way is a different matter. With the rise of mass communication people have become more critical than earlier generations about the messages they receive and trust. Opinion leaders must handle their fragile asset with great care. If they do not manage to come across as sincere, or if they "sell" themselves for commercial purposes too often, or change their minds too much, their credibility will soon subside. No wonder, then, that opinion leaders only manage to win over large groups when it is clear to those groups that their opinion is based on true enthusiasm. Only the superpromoters among their numbers will manage to maintain their credibility. There is, however, another aspect of new age media: it is getting easier all the time to become an opinion leader. Anyone can start up a blog or leave a trail of opinions across several online forums. All you need is time, pertinent knowledge and a healthy dose of sincerity.

IN CONCLUSION ... AND PEEKING FORWARD

We met the superpromoter in this chapter; someone who influences others with their enthusiasm. We've seen that spreading enthusiasm can result in exponential growth. Another positive aspect of superpromoters is that they can teach you what you're doing right, which can build your self-confidence and inspires you with positive energy.

Superpromoters come in different guises. Approximately 20% of the Dutch population can be classified as "natural born" superpromoters. Then there are the situational superpromoters, people who spread their enthusiasm within a particular category of products only. We were also introduced to the antipromoter, someone who is (has become) exceptionally negative about a business or company and advises everyone to avoid all forms of contact.

The next chapter will take a look at an evolution in thinking about customer orientation. This is a development that covers a wide spectrum from satisfaction-measurement to superpromoter engagement.

3

AN EVOLUTION IN CUSTOMER ORIENTATION

INTRODUCTION

Customer demand a century ago was basically determined by what was being produced in factories. Mass production had arrived, courtesy of the Industrial Revolution, and strong demand for those products rendered unnecessary any form of focus on whether customer were in fact pleased with these products. Today the competition for customers is much greater and most blue-collar workers have traded up to white collars by earning their money in the service industry. Citing the global economy as a culprit, it has become more and more difficult to maintain a high degree of competitive differentiation for specific products on offer, or to be the consistent low-price supplier, for that matter. In our economic environment, labor, raw materials and other means of production are in ready supply to most producers. Successful companies know how to combine a competitively priced and good product with customer satisfaction. It has become increasingly difficult to remain successful in the long term if one excels in only one of the following areas.[17]

Product leadership

Products are being developed at breakneck speed and copied by the competition even faster. This trend has made it virtually impossible to maintain a competitive advantage over the long term based only on product innovation.

Price leadership

Potential profit margins are trending toward convergence as the global economy increasingly makes product inputs available to all suppliers on the same basis. This also makes it harder to earn adequate profits over the long term only by offering the lowest price.

Leader in customer orientation

Because product and price leadership become harder to achieve, a company's ability to stick out from the crowd with a differentiated product will more and more depend on their level of customer orientation. The one area where businesses have the best opportunity to distinguish themselves lies in customer satisfaction. However, superior customer satisfaction only becomes relevant when the product being offered is of the right quality and its price competitive.

The intention of this chapter of *The Superpromoter* is to demonstrate that companies that take customer orientation all the way are companies that will excel at all of the three areas just mentioned. They will be differentiating themselves by providing superior customer satisfaction, while being able to offer the most innovative products with the highest quality, and have some of the best profit margins in the business to top it off!

What we will be describing during this chapter can best be described as an evolution in the thinking about customer orientation. This evolution is currently well underway and can be expected to accelerate over the coming years. The first step down this evolutionary path is about listening to customers and about striving to make them happy. Many companies have already taken this first step, or are preparing to take it soon. They are focused on keeping their customers happy, and often also on strengthening customer loyalty. Although this may seem to be a noble pursuit – which it is – the quest for a loyal and satisfied clientele is not sufficiently ambitious to be seen as a seriously differentiating proposition. The life span of the average customer relationship is too short, while the competition for a "satisfied clientele" is too great for this to be an adequate or acceptable objective. Organizations that recognize this fact have usually progressed to at least the second step on the long march of evolution. They are working hard to make their customers enthusiastic for their products or services, since they understand full well that customer enthusiasm makes all the difference in their own success. When businesses, and any other types of organization are ready to take the third step they start to concentrate their efforts on lining up superpromoters. They realize that superpromoters in particular are the ones who can influence their social networks. When they get to know their superpromoters well, they can adapt their organizations to permit these superpromoters the scope to do what they do best: superpromoting, of course! Finally, the organization becomes aligned to help create superpromoters, to nurture them and help them transfer their enthusiasm on to others.

EVOLUTIONARY STEP # 1: STRIVING FOR SATISFIED AND LOYAL CUSTOMERS

Listening to customers is the first step down the road of customer orientation that any business has to take. Admittedly this may sound like we are belaboring the obvious, but the large number of businesses out there that have not yet taken this first step suggests otherwise. Their reasons for not taking this step can be several. Here are a few:

Having a monopoly

If you are a monopolist, there is an increased likelihood that your corporate culture does not have much of a customer focus. Without competitive pressure, how would any company resist the temptation to become complacent and lazy? Your customers have no alternative for you to worry about. We often encounter this attitude among recently privatized government institutions. Happily, these entities are now also among those most involved in developing a culture of customer focus.

Size and organizational structure

Some companies have become such behemoths, such bureaucracies, that they are no longer in touch with their customers. Sometimes this happens when the end-user purchases the products through an intermediary. Insurance companies, selling insurance policies through brokers are a typical example where the actual customer, the insured party, is no longer on their radar screen. In other cases, where the business is still dealing with customers, it is company management that has lost touch with its staff, the ones selling its products to real people. The link between senior management and customer is entirely lost. Where that has happened, expect to find an ivory tower running the business, blind to customer needs or satisfaction.

Primarily focused on selling

Unfortunately, there are still too many businesses that are only concentrated on hauling in new customers, yet once they are in the bag unable to give them any useful attention. Their reward system is based on the sales force meeting or exceeding new-customer targets; no wonder many a sales pitch has an extremely tenuous relationship with truth or fact! Why should they care? Their objective is growing their customer base, not keeping customers (happy). And so, many unhappy customers will exit through the revolving door at their first opportunity, never to return again.

No wonder, then, that it would be a huge step for some companies to start looking after the happiness of their customers. Although those that have not yet taken this first step would benefit from improving their customer-satisfaction scores, I would nevertheless encourage them to skip that evolutionary first step, urging them instead to risk a hop, skip and jump to the third step down our evolutionary path. During the course of this chapter it will become clear why this is so. The third step involves our superpromoter...

Aiming for (dis)satisfied Customers

How well companies are able to do things – their processing quality, you might say – has traditionally been measured by customer satisfaction. This is familiar terrain: *Did they provide us with an informative quotation? Do they answer the phone on time? Are their products any good?* If the quality control system were working as it should, then a low score on one of these measurements would result in action being taken for "improvement". Followed by a check to see if the improvement worked, and if it didn't, a new "improvement" will be implemented. Aiming for satisfied customers in this manner is seen as an inherent component of quality control systems. Sounds sensible and useful, don't you think? Unfortunately not a lot of positive energy is released, if all you are doing is aiming for satisfaction. There are many managers who've been complaining for years that client satisfaction scores are hard to interpret, while getting the score to move even harder. One quarter it goes up a percent or two, the next quarter it goes down again a little. Another, somewhat interesting, complaint is that there appears to be no relationship between satisfaction and a firm's financial performance.

There is, however, an even more fundamental problem to be addressed when you are "aiming for satisfaction"; something that normally doesn't get a lot of attention. It is that "aiming for satisfaction" really means "aiming for dissatisfaction". The reason is as follows. Quality control systems designed to improve customer relations are in fact aimed at removing customer dissatisfaction. The nature of these types of systems is to focus the attention on everything that goes wrong. However relevant this might be, if people are continuously being told what they are doing wrong in their jobs, you might expect them to become thoroughly demoralized and be lacking in motivation. We should take a cue from how we raise our children! We all know that in raising a child the most important thing is to tell them what they are doing well and not to concentrate too much attention on what they might be doing wrong. Positive feedback works best. That's how you help them to gain their self-confidence and they become enthusiastic, resulting in the desired behavior being repeated.

The same rule applies to animals, of all kinds. Take orcas[18] for example, also known as killer whales. Trying to teach them something by using punishment is completely useless; try it, and you're lucky if the orca does not get annoyed and seeks to remove its gadfly. If, on the other hand, you consistently reward an orca for desired behavior you can teach them the most amazing things. You'll know what I mean if you have ever been to a killer whale show. While our children are still tiny, we know how to apply this didactic principle pretty much automatically. We don't scold babies for throwing up all over us, but when they smile for the first time, we fall all over ourselves complimenting them with this early step down the road of becoming a fully functioning human being. It gets harder not to correct children too much as they get older, but modern parenting is keen on pats-on-the-back as the motivator of choice. When children get to adolescence, positive feedback tends to drop off sharply. They come home from school with a report card filled with top grades…and one fail. Guess where all the attention is focused! And then, off to work: there are no more compliments in store for junior; he's in the real world now. Employees will always be told what they are doing wrong, but hardly ever get complimented for the things they do right. Positive feedback is not something to expect from a quality control system, nor from most personnel evaluations, either. There, the best you can usually hope for is the absence of remarks like, "such and such improvements are needed" on your evaluation sheet. Clearly, it means that the clients aren't sufficiently dissatisfied, nor is your boss sufficiently disappointed, to be giving you any feedback at all. So, *not* getting negative feedback, for many workers, is about the best they can hope for in terms of appreciation for their effort. In conclusion, in growing up we're being programmed to give and get negative feedback in the ordinary course of business.

Another problem with "satisfaction" is that most satisfaction-criteria tend to be rooted in rationality. Things like price/quality/delivery speed/complaints-handling are all typical – yet rational – aspects of the ordinary client relationship. Not that these things aren't important; they are! But the reasons for people becoming and remaining customers are not often that rational. There are other emotional or social factors, which can play a huge role. Often, these things are not fully understood by the customers themselves, either.

Aiming for Customer Loyalty

Customer loyalty tends to have many different definitions. In *The Superpromoter* customer loyalty means the extent to which customers intend to remain loyal customers in the future or, if we are talking about the purchase of products, the extent to which they intend to repeat their purchases. Now, we should ask ourselves, is it wise to be aiming for customer loyalty? Just as was the case with customer satisfaction, it represents a great step forward for a company that hitherto had been neglecting customer loyalty entirely. If you are aiming for customer loyalty, it is important to understand the reasons behind their loyalty; there could be any number of reasons. Here are five definitions of customer loyalty:

1. Calculative loyalty: These are customers who remain loyal because they perceive it to be in their best rational-economic interests. They make a cost-benefit analysis, comparing one business to its competition, and will remain loyal as long as they see that as being to their advantage. As soon as the competition offers a better deal the calculative customer switches.

2. Forced loyalty (or negative calculative loyalty): These are customers who are being loyal for lack of alternatives. Even if they did wish to switch, it would not be possible, or at least would be very difficult, frightening or something stoutly resisted by the customer for whatever reason.

3. Normative loyalty: A customer whose loyalty is based on the belief that a specific supplier offers a superior quality. This customer desires to do business with the best supplier and believes his current one offers the highest quality.

4. Affective loyalty: This customer is being made to feel good by the supplier, hence their loyalty. There exists an emotional connection between the two, and the customer values that fact greatly. This type of emotional connection might be based on personal ties and may also have a social or historical context.

5. Traditional loyalty: Habit is what makes this customer loyal. No reason for switching existed till now, or at least the customer didn't feel like thinking about it. This category includes those customers that have had a long-term relationship with their supplier, but not necessarily having a strong tie.

Calculative Loyalty

To the grower or manufacturer of energy intensive products their utility represents a serious cost. Therefore it makes sense to cost-compare all energy suppliers regularly to make sure that the lowest cost supplier is being used. This is known as having calculative loyalty toward the energy supplier.

Forced loyalty

Not having a drivers' license will make any person – perhaps reluctantly – a customer of public transportation. Assuming they have a need to travel, of course. Similarly, an entrepreneur could feel trapped by his accountant because switching to another would be too much of a pain or the risks would feel too great. Customers not making a switch because of a perceived lack of choice are defined as having "forced loyalty".

Normative loyalty

A large company is hauled into court regularly on suspicion of committing the ecological crime of environmental pollution. If found guilty, this could cost the company both a fortune and its reputation. The company therefore maintains a relationship with a specialized law firm that has the best reputation in this area. As long as that reputation stays intact the company will continue to be their loyal client. This we call normative loyalty.

Affective loyalty

As a small boy this person used to go to the same resort, which therefore carries fond memories for him. Although his parents have long since died, he still takes his family there at least once a year. For this particular resort he clearly has deep emotional ties. We call this affective loyalty.

Traditional loyalty

When a large market with often complex products is opened up to competition – think of private health insurance in Holland recently, or telephone companies a few decades before – an interesting phenomenon occurs that only a very small percentage of customers make a switch because the majority cannot be bothered to investigate what is on offer from new entrants. It is more than likely that they would be able to get a better deal elsewhere, but they are put off by the effort involved in switching. This is what we call traditional loyalty.

Why do we actually want to know what type of loyalty a client may have? Because the different types of loyalty are related to the enthusiasm of a superpromoter and it is also connected to the degree in which they are inclined to share that enthusiasm. Which of these forms of loyalty are most common among superpromoters? They are unlikely to tell us that a traditional or forced loyalty tie is the most important reason for their remaining a customer. Any customer telling us he's only there as a customer because he cannot be bothered to make a switch is just not suf-ficiently enthusiastic. This group of customers who feel trapped into being loyal will contain the highest num-ber of antipromoters. They will become very frustrated, especially when dissatisfied, with the notion of being tied to one supplier. And they will certainly be warning others not to do business with them if they can avoid it.

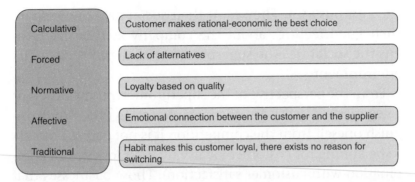

Calculative	Customer makes rational-economic the best choice
Forced	Lack of alternatives
Normative	Loyalty based on quality
Affective	Emotional connection between the customer and the supplier
Traditional	Habit makes this customer loyal, there exists no reason for switching

Figure 3.1 Different forms of customer loyalty

The managing director who is unhappy with his bankers, but does not have the courage to sever the relationship because of the financial risks it would entail, will nonetheless be discouraging everyone he knows from doing business with them. Calculative Loyalists are unlikely to be superpromoters either, unless very excited about the price and if they believe that the offer is very attractive for the people of their social circle.

Most superpromoters will be found in the normative or affective category. Customers are going to be enthusiastic when they feel they are doing business with the best guys on the block, or when they believe that they've just purchased the highest quality possible. It makes it much easier for a customer to recommend a certain company in these circumstances, mainly because they can be reasonably certain that it will not end in disappointment for the person they are giving the recommendation to. Among customers who have a strong emotional tie to a brand or business there will be a large number of superpromoters. Their affective loyalty causes them to wish the company well and is the reason they like to support it with their enthusiasm. They want their social network to share their good feelings about the company as this strengthens the social ties the superpromoter has with their social environment.

From the perspective of the superpromoter these different categories of loyalty are of some interest. In order to distinguish oneself from the competition it is not enough merely to be aiming for customer loyalty by itself (or even in combination with customer satisfaction). Those businesses that want to stick out from the crowd because of their customer orientation will need at the very least to take the second step down our path of evolution.

EVOLUTIONARY STEP # 2: AIMING FOR ENTHUSIASM

To some extent you could compare the relationship between customer and supplier to a love affair. Sometimes it's love at first sight. Sometimes it lasts beyond sell-by, and love has worn a bit thin; perhaps the time has come to fast forward to the end of the affair and look for something new and exiting. That's when bottled up resentments and simmering angers can explode into something large and unpleasant. Sometimes love is blind and while you're soaring among the stars this leads to unbridled enthusiasm. Is all of this really necessary to explain...? Of course not. Everyone knows about the ups and downs of love's highways and byways. All of us have a pretty good idea what it's like during those moments of supreme happiness or sadness. So, let's leave it to the poets to talk of love; we'll stick to our topic here.

But...why are we choosing this moment to compare a commercial activity with love? Because organizations and businesses, during the second stage in their evolutionary journey toward client focus, concentrate their efforts on customers who have fallen in love with their products or services; someone in love with his or her car, for example, or the friend who is proudly showing off her new TV. It might be the person who just received some super service (remember the honeymooners flying KLM?). Like lovers, they beam with eagerness and talk passionately about brands or products that have fired their enthusiasm.

Word-of-mouth behavior as a way of expressing enthusiasm

Word-of-mouth behavior is clearly a pretty major component of social behavior. Of course it's social: once we get excited about something we love to share that thing we are wild about with others. By recommending something to somebody, we are trying to give them valuable advice about the thing that has ignited our enthusiasms. It is not just the enthusiasm itself that causes us to go and tell our friends. Whether consciously or not, we are seeking to boost their esteem for us. Helping someone with valuable advice can also raise our social standing. No wonder we are doing this all the time! As an experiment, pay attention to conversations going on around you next time you're at the hairdresser's or in the waiting room at the dentist's. You'd be amazed at how much word-of-mouth recommending is involved. And that is apart from the professional advice you're getting about hair gel or enamel-friendly toothpaste. Spontaneous word-of-mouth is a nearly universal feature of social exchange.

Word-of-mouth observed in a hair salon

1. A recommendation for a particular holiday destination:

"We took the kids to this Theme Park for the weekend, they really loved it. I'm sure that yours would love it too..."

2. A recommendation for a favorite TV series:

"Hey, if you liked Dancing with the Stars while you were in the US, you've got to see Strictly Come Dancing now you're back in Britain...!"

3. A recommendation for getting a watch strap repaired:

"If I were you, I'd just go to that jeweler's round the corner from here, I bet they would repair it for you for nothing ..."

Surely, word-of-mouth behavior is as much a part of the social landscape as talking about the weather, or asking after somebody's health. The difference is probably that the latter two won't have the same economic impact. Ebay, Autotrader or Abebooks – all online marketplaces – are all being used by people who were recommended to the site by someone else. Take a Dutch site, Marktplaats – Market Place – the name says it all, as an example. Word of mouth made them so popular that Ebay was willing to pay € 225 million for them in 2004. They hardly ever used any form of advertising other than word of mouth...powerful stuff, that!

Successful online sites are thriving on word-of-mouth behavior and many have it as their central business focus. Like the restaurant guides and B&B reviews; most businesses have bought into the idea of having their customers make recommendations – Amazon proves it works – and many customers will read those book reviews or take a look at a restaurant guide before deciding where to eat. And again, all of these sites live on word-of-mouth recommendations themselves. There is no doubt that the internet has given a serious boost to enthusiastic word-of-mouthers.

Do you deserve to be recommended?

The urge to make a recommendation about a company can evaporate quickly if something doesn't feel right with them. When something doesn't sit well or feel comfortable, these uneasy feelings can be hidden just beneath the surface and be something the client isn't even fully aware of. We often see evidence that these feelings only come to light when you dig deeper than usual. There appears to be a direct correlation between feeling appreciated on the one side and having the desire to make a recommendation on the other. Obvious, really: who is going to recommend any outfit that causes you to feel unappreciated? Here is an example taken from an interview with someone working for the government legal department of a large town. He indicated his satisfaction with the law firm they used and thought that his department would continue using the firm for the foreseeable future. When we asked him if he would recommend them to someone else, he had to stop and think for a while and then said no. That was a surprise! So we asked him why he would not recommend a firm he was satisfied with. He confirmed he was basically quite pleased with the work the firm had done for him and that their legal advice was always of good quality. He also appreciated that they were able to lighten his workload, but that this was also where the problem lurked.

The law firm was a very determined "load lightener" and our interviewee felt pushed aside by them every time these "gentlemen" were doing work for his department. He said he sometimes got the feeling that they saw him as "that little civil servant" who shouldn't worry himself too much about what the big boys were up to. A classic example of someone who does not feel appreciated, most would say! And yet, the law firm never knew what was going on, nor did the lawyers realize what the consequences of their behavior was going to be. What was clear from the interview was that the law firm was missing out on clients because this particular government employee was not recommending them. When he would talk to other departments, who worked with other law firms, he would never recommend them to his lawyers. He basically did not think they deserved it! And the existing framework agreement made no difference to him...

Enthusiasm does not automatically result in word of mouth

Part of what makes word of mouth so powerful is that it represents a sincere expression of enthusiasm. Most every business – hopefully – gets to deal with enthusiastic customers, but this enthusiasm does not always translate into word-of-mouth behavior. Let us take a closer look at other means of expressing enthusiasm in the section.

Some products might not be recommended very readily because the enthusiast would rather not see other people start using them as well. A good example would be new clothes. You could be enthusiastic about your new blouse for example, but wouldn't want your colleague at work to get the same thing right away. Your enthusiasm will find a different way of expressing itself to your network. If you are very happy with the way you're dressed and happen to be someone others like to follow, then they will be emulating the way you're dressed anyway. By wearing those clothes you are walking advertisement for them. Yet fashionable trendsetters do not actively recommend their clothes. If everybody starts wearing their clothes they'll have to go out and buy themselves a new outfit if they are to hang on to their trendsetter status. Even if you're not actively promoting your wardrobe by word of mouth, it's still a drain on the wallet to be cool. Enthusiasm does not always express itself as a recommendation to others....

In the following situations enthusiasm tends to be expressed differently.

Scarcity

We have already compared client relationships to love affairs. The comparison breaks down when looking at word-of-mouth behavior. There's something wrong if your lover is recommending you to friends and acquaintances! Scarcity value is the reason why word of mouth doesn't work in love. The people you are in love with are a scarce product and if you want to keep something for yourself you aren't going to recommend it to others. The same applies to products and services. The scarcer they are the less likely you will be to recommend them. Take babysitters, for example. Very hard to come by reliable and good ones, and if you find a good one you are not likely to be telling everybody. The more people are making use of "your" babysitter the less she'll be available for you when you need her one evening.

Recommending your babysitter to your friends is a dangerous thing to do.

Monopoly

There is no need for word of mouth if you're dealing with a monopoly. When you need to get a new passport, you don't ask for recommendations on where to get one. There is only one place to go. That also means that passport suppliers do not need to generate word of mouth on their hot new product. The people staffing the passport counter would do better to aim for customer satisfaction. Following this line of reasoning a little further, one might define people very satisfied with the way they were treated at the passport office as "enthusiasts". Satisfaction is a good measuring tool, but only those who have expressed themselves to be "very" satisfied could truly be called enthusiasts. But some monopolies should consider whether there is, or needs to be, any desire to make recommendations for their product. Although National Railways tend to have an almost absolute monopoly on train transportation, it is good to remember Theodore Leavitt's *Marketing Myopia*[19], written in 1960, where it was made clear that rail transportation is not the same as transportation in general: beware who your competitor might be! It is relevant to know if train travelers intend to recommend that form of transportation to their friends and acquaintances over other means of transportation. The monopoly of the railways is at its shakiest when dealing with the movement of people. Cars, buses, bicycles, planes: they are all their competition. A good measure of train travelers' enthusiasm for that mode of transportation is when they are telling their friends with cars to take the train.

Low degree of involvement

Some products generate less involvement from their users than others. As we have mentioned before, finance or insurance products and services fall into this category. These are not the kind of products many people would choose to talk about in day-to-day social intercourse as compared to products that do attract that type of involvement. These might include the type of products that are "fun" and cause people to spend time talking about them, such as music, holidays, electronic gadgets, cars and so on. Products that have a low degree of involvement from their users are normally only recommended when people ask for specific advice (passive recommendation).

Taboo products

People do not like to talk about some products much, or at all. These are for example products that deal with physical ailments. I've been upset many times in my life by finding the wrong pimple at the wrong time in the wrong place. This usually happens under the unflattering glare of bathroom lights. At some point in time during my student days Clearasil introduced a new product to the market. When I tried it for the first time I promptly developed a odd skin rash, so I wrote to the company to complain. It turned out later that my skin condition had nothing to do with Clearasil, it was the result of too much chlorine in my local swimming pool. The company, however, immediately responded to my letter and sent me a questionnaire to try and find out what was going on. They also sent me three bottles of the old product. I thought that was pretty good, as responses go, and as I seem to remember I was pretty enthusiastic about the company. But I never recommended Clearasil to other people. In fact, I never talked about this subject. Clearasil was not part of the locker room conversation among my male friends, and with women I tried to keep as far away as I could from ever discussing anything to do with pimples.

Specific industries

For some industries, such as the Fast Moving Consumer Goods (FMCG) industry, or the fashion industry, word of mouth is less important than it is in other industries. People don't usually go around actively recommending that you try a product like chewing gum or a soft drink. At least not in an outspoken manner. Herd behavior is often the important influence for these product categories. What the cool kids are drinking is likely to be copied by those who want to be one of those cool cats. But herd behavior in these circumstances is more of an expression of enthusiasm than of word-of-mouth recommendations.

We have seen that enthusiastic customers are not always planning to make recommendations. So, what are the indicators of their enthusiasm? Perhaps we should be looking for other indicators of their enthusiasm, such as measuring satisfaction or loyalty. It is possible to measure enthusiasm in this manner. People indicating that they are "very" happy or that they will "definitely" remain as customers, are also displaying some form of enthusiasm. That is pretty much always the case when they start using words such as "very" or "most" or "definitively"...at least if it is used to describe something positive. When we start hearing that a customer is "very" dissatisfied, this is the typically negative attitude to be found among antipromoters. When the desire to make recommendations is not an expression of enthusiasm, then aiming for satisfied customers is the superior alternative.

Herd behavior as a result of visible enthusiasm

Mankind is constantly copying. There are two emotions in particular that can strongly provoke herd behavior: fear and enthusiasm. In a panic everybody starts running after the same person, but enthusiasm, too, is prone to be copied. People, who are visibly excited or happy with their product, are going to be copied by others, whether deliberately or not. It is very easy to observe this behavior among children. If one child gets an ice cream and is happy, then the next one wants to have an ice cream and be happy as well. But if the ice cream does not meet with an enthusiastic reception (it happens!) then the other children will also show less interest. The fact that we learn how better to suppress this explicit expression of envy as grown-ups does not mean that the emotion has also been suppressed. We too want to have the things that others show they are happy with. We won't always be conscious of the envy inside us waking up our desires, but the new desire has surely been registered at some conscious level and will influence our purchasing behavior as soon as we are given an opportunity.

Enthusiasm: Powerful yet Undervalued

Enthusiasm, everybody would agree, is a phenomenon that is both positive and powerful. In comparison, mere "satisfaction" is really quite flat and lacking in energy. The etymology of "to satisfy" suggests "to make enough"...but not much more. Content...satisfied...OK...are all expressions that, although somewhat positive, create no sparkle. And positive with a sparkle is what we need in an economy where people, products and processes are moving at ever-increasing speed and consumers are more critical than ever before in recorded history. A merely contented consumer is open to all offers a competitor can throw at them, and surely not one making recommendations anytime soon. To excel, it must be your mission to create as many enthusiastic consumers as possible.

The funny thing is, however, that enthusiastic customers are not paid a great deal of attention in most organizations and businesses. Their attention is usually trained on the dissatisfied ones. Those companies that have already taken the first step toward customer orientation will normally have a complaints procedure in place. If the issue is big enough, someone from management can always go and talk to the unhappy client. But how do enthusiastic customers get to tell their stories? We have looked, but don't know of any business enterprise that has opened up an enthusiasm hotline in addition to its complaints number or helpline. When's the last time a manager went to visit an enthusiastic client? This seems odd, particularly since talking to enthusiastic customers is much nicer, and more useful from a strategic point of view. So, why is it that enthusiastic customers are being ignored at all levels? There is a very fundamental answer. We all ignore enthusiasm because we are programmed that way! All of our focus is on improving things that go wrong, we've never learned to focus on the things that are going well. Our basic thinking is that everything will be all right if we are able to make small, incremental improvements to those things we don't do all that well yet. And that is exactly what happens, of course! Things get improved a little and most of it is ambling along quite well. But don't expect sparkle, powerful or wow! It is distinctly possible that at some point the important people in your life, your teachers, customers, boss and many more will be satisfied. The question is whether that will be good enough for you...

We hope the message is getting through: enthusiastic customers deserve more attention. This by no means suggests we should ignore customer satisfaction or loyalty issues. It can be an interesting exercise to compare different aspects of a customer relationship with each other in an effort to understand them at a deeper level. During the honeymoon phase this type of comparative analysis is probably not necessary. When, however, the relationship begins to show some signs of wear and tear, a more thorough analysis, possibly with professional therapy, could be most instructive. If that relationship cannot even be salvaged with therapy – love's a delicate flower, after all – then perhaps the wisdom gained from failure will assist the next relationship in blooming longer.

Let's not lose sight of our objective: to create enthusiastic customers rather than reduce levels of dissatisfaction. Clearly, unhappy customers who nevertheless have the potential of becoming enthusiasts do deserve attention. Giving grumbling customers the right kind of attention is a great opportunity for turning them into enthusiastic ones. And this is what "aiming for enthusiasm" really means. So, a complaint is really an opportunity to win over a new enthusiast. The fact that a customer makes the effort to complain suggests that they are prepared to make the effort to remain a customer. Handling that complaint effectively can turn the experience around into something positive. Those customers who remain dissatisfied after you have done everything reasonable in your power to make them happy are perhaps better served by being advised to find another product or service. Perhaps a well-meant recommendation of that nature will allow you to part as friends: the best deal you could make under the circumstances. The energy that this releases can then be poured into other, more enthusiastic customers. One dissatisfied customer who requires particular attention is the one who was enthusiastic before, but no longer is. It is important to know why their enthusiasm was lost and learn what you can from this, and then to do everything you can to win their enthusiasm back. Being ignored is about the worst thing that can happen to formerly enthusiastic customers: it will really make them disappointed!

EVOLUTIONARY STEP #3: AIMING FOR SUPERPROMOTERS

Superpromoters are enthusiastic customers, who share their enthusiasm and thereby exercise influence on their social network. The distinction between a promoter and a superpromoter lies in their transfer of enthusiasm and the influence it has on others. This is an important and crucial distinction for the success of a product or business. If a business has many promoters but not many superpromoters, it means that the company has a large group of enthusiastic, and probably also loyal, customers, but they are not setting new customers alight. The implication is that the company has to recruit every new customer themselves. Since this is how it has been done for centuries it is not an impossible task. Yet, this way is becoming harder by the day, because it is harder to reach potential new clients through traditional marketing and sales channels. With many superpromoters among your ranks, sales and marketing runs on autopilot, which is not only more effective but also cheaper. Businesses that get to know their superpromoters well, and discover how to lever their superpromoting assets, gain a significant competitive advantage, or may even knock their competitors out of the race entirely. They can do this by collaborating with their superpromoters to develop products or services for which there isn't any competition within miles. Here are a few reasons for collaborating with your superpromoters.

Superpromoters as turnover generators

Fred Reichheld[20], among others, was able to demonstrate the causative correlation between word-of-mouth behavior and sales growth. A joint research project between Blauw Research and the Erasmus Universiteit Rotterdam[21] has also identified this correlation. Within groups of customers who demonstrate stronger word-of-mouth behavior – promoters – it is the superpromoters in particular who procure new customers. That is what superpromoters do: they persuade people to become your clients.

Superpromoters as guardians of the soul

You might say that entrepreneurs are really the ultimate superpromoters. They, after all, are so enthusiastic about an idea that they formed a company to spread their idea as far and wide as they could. They are expecting enough other people to get as enthusiastic about the idea that they will start buying their product. New ventures are only successful if the new idea catches on, for which enthusiasm is crucial. Together with the entrepreneur, enthusiastic customers to some extent also make up the soul of a company. This is because they are the guardians of the original reason for the company's existence, not just because they are sales boosters who buy the products, or indirectly because of their word-of-mouth enthusiasm. When businesses grow, their founders often experience how they are growing further apart from their customers and products because they spend more time managing the business. It is not unusual for founders to disappear from the scene altogether, increasing the chance that the original reason for starting their company fades into the background and their unique and original character evaporates. Nonetheless, among superpromoters there should still be that original enthusiasm that was alive among the founders when they began. These superpromoters could be customers, but could also be people working for the company. If you hear them talk it becomes clear once more why the business got started in the first place. Companies that manage to hang on to their soul are more successful over the longer term.[22] Superpromoters reflect that soul and are its guardian angels. If the business checks its reflection in this mirror regularly it will stay on course.

Superpromoters as visionaries

The first chapter sketched a picture of the superpromoter standing in the bow of a ship. This picture is particularly appropriate to those rapidly developing companies where the superpromoters approve of or even expect great speed. They are the ones who frequently are the first to identify new opportunities in the market. These are the people who can tell us what we have to do to be the first to seize the opportunity. However, their innovative powers do not only stem from being among the group who are the first users of new products. You can be a superpromoter without always needing to be an early adopter. They can be very enthusiastic about a new product or service without the slightest desire to be among the first to try it out. Their visionary powers derive particularly from their collective knowledge of their social network. Whether consciously or subconsciously, superpromoters analyze huge amounts of information on a daily basis about their social environment. One might say they are their own market researchers, becoming experts at opinions and the people around them. This doesn't mean that any given superpromoter will necessarily represent exactly the right target audience for a given product. But all of them together should have a pretty good idea of their social reality. There is a principle at work here that is described well in *The Wisdom of Crowds*[23]. Its author, James Surowiecky describes how a crowd of people can be capable of making fairly complex assessments. An auditorium full of students can make an accurate guesstimate of the number of beans – give or take a bean – kept in a jar. Any random group of people online can predict which politician will win an election. The average estimation is eerily accurate time and again, provided a few conditions are met. The group of people must be diverse, and its members should not be in direct contact with each other. If a group of superpromoters meet these criteria they can be potently

95

useful in observing trends looming just below the horizon. They know what gets them going and know if their social circle will share their enthusiasm. By and large, superpromoters are very social beings who find it essential to share their enthusiasms with friends. If a new idea excites nobody in their environment, the superpromoter's enthusiasm will also wane. Because of their extensive experience in searching for new products or ideas that can make them and others enthusiastic, superpromoters develop a keen sense of what will be a success and what will not. A very valuable crystal ball for any company to be able to gaze into…

Superpromoters as source of energy

We've all experienced how good it can feel to be complimented on something that you think is important. It might be your prowess as a sportsman, your draughtsmanship, or how you look. Forgive me if this sounds too New Agey, but at times like this you can feel energy flowing into your body. Compliments fuel positive energy. As a source of energy, compliments are underestimated by many a teacher, parent or manager. It is a tired story, we get to hear what's wrong much more often than compliments for what we might be doing right. Our customer relationships tend to operate on the same principle. An enthusiastic customer is much more likely to talk about it to his friends than to the company. The same applies to disappointments. But if that unhappy client were to complain to the company, the employee involved would undoubtedly be told about it. But positive feedback from enthusiastic clients is very unlikely to find its way to the employee most responsible. Most companies don't seem to have a procedure in place for addressing this phenomenon and most managers are looking for the things that need improvement. Improvements are born from negative feedback. And the unfortunate result is that energy-sapping negative feedback is much more prominent than energy-rich positive feedback. When businesses allow their superpromoters to speak and allow employees to listen, motivation gets a welcome boost. Superpromoters don't just praise, they also talk positively with others about their experiences, so they tell us. This can be a wonderful experience for the company's employees: it becomes clear to them that others find their labors useful, and that they are really making people enthusiastic about what they are doing on a daily basis. It is a pity and a waste to leave that an untapped source of energy.

The superpromoter as critical friend

Positive feedback is not the only thing you may expect from a superpromoter. In fact, they will be the first to tell you when something is going wrong. Yet, this form of negative feedback is less energy depleting than other types of negative feedback that may land on your doorstep from other customers. Criticism coming from a superpromoter can best be compared to that which you might be given by a good friend when you are doing something wrong or something is not working as it should. Imagine you've bought something to wear that makes you look utterly ridiculous. Most people would laugh at you behind your back, or will look away with some embarrassment. But a good friend will warn you and tell you to go and put on something else. And that would be doubly true if the friend also happens to be a superpromoter, because they are not lacking in social skills and are used to exercising their influence in any case. Definitively handy characteristics to have if you have to be the one to point out a painful mistake to someone. That, after all, is what good friends are for; they make the effort because they have your best interests at heart. That kind of motivation to tell you what you might be doing wrong is also less hurtful.

The customer who happens to be a superpromoter has similar motivations to be critical, as a good friend would have. They want things to go well for the company because thy feel involved and their desire to remain enthusiastic, something they also want to be able to continue sharing with their social network. If the company's level of service starts to show hairline cracks, it will be harder for them to share their enthusiasms, since it increases the risk that their disappointed friends would cause their reputation as a reliable enthusiast to suffer. Prompt improvement of these points is the only ticket back to being enthusiastic without reserve. Therefore companies must stay focused on improving. Preferably on those areas of improvement that have been suggested to them by their superpromoters. They will know quite well how to improve the product or service in such a way that would make their social network enthusiastic, or at least contented. Second, you must take the antipromoter seriously. Where one may compare a critical superpromoter to a good friend giving you helpful advice, the antipromoter, on the other hand, could be seen as a disgruntled ex. Of course, sometimes those ex-friends have become so disappointed that their criticisms seem to be more an expression of emotional disquiet than of purposeful criticism, however valuable it may be. It can be used to discover, for example, how to prevent superpromoters from becoming antipromoters, or whether the antipromoter can be returned to the fold, or whether the damage they can do to your reputation can be contained. In addition to antipromoters, some customers just like to complain because they're just negative about everything; often their frustrations are not about something within your control. It's a bit of a snare to spend too much time and attention on this group, since they are not serving your best interests…never did and never will. Quite a contrast with superpromoters, who will know all the important things to work on, and be happy to help you decide how to tackle them. Superpromoters, after all, are also co-creators.

The superpromoter as a cost-saving strategy

Successful businesses are capable of doing things more effectively and for less money. If superpromoters can be marshaled in a meaningful manner, they can produce significant cost-savings in several areas while increasing the company's effectiveness.

Cost saving # 1: Marketing expenses
Superpromoters are doing your marketing for free.[24] They are enthusiasts by nature and love to tell their friends about the things that make them enthusiastic. If they were not doing it for free their authenticity would be lost; the superpromoters' sincere enthusiasm is their most effective marketing tool. If harnessed effectively, their efforts could save you significantly on marketing expense, or at least make use of the budget a lot smarter.

Cost saving # 2: Sales
Once the superpromoters get going they will take over your sales job for you as well. One of the video clips available

on *www.superpromoters.nl* shows a woman who is sharing her enthusiasm for Trollbeads beaded bracelets. At some point she is describing how she praises Trollbeads to her friends and acquaintances. The interviewer asks her what the conversations with her friends are usually like when she's talking about Trollbeads. We are then treated to her enthusiastic description of a typical conversation with one of her girlfriends:

> *"So, I'm telling her about it full of enthusiasm...". "But it's sooo expensive!", sighs my friend. To which I reply, "But it's not too bad, really...If you first buy the beginners' set, you can then grow your collection slowly...". "I should be working for them", she says to the interviewer, laughing.*

The woman tells us that six more in her social circle have already bought Trollbeads products owing to her enthusiasm. And then her colleagues and boyfriend have bought her Trollbeads as a present because that was what she asked for. If you were to have several of these kinds of superpromoters we know how fast you would be growing: 6 x 6 x 6 x 6 x 6 x 6 x 6 x 6 x 6 x 6 = more than 60 million new customers. Commenting on the video clip, a Trollbeads product manager told us that the brand is being sold pretty much exclusively through word of mouth and has become very popular in a short period of time. I wonder how many salespeople would have been needed to reach the same sales numbers without word-of-mouth advertising doing its job for them.

Cost saving # 3: Research and Development
The fact that superpromoters can be ideal co-creators has been mentioned earlier. A number of them love to be early

adopters; the first on the block with the latest. Not only do they know a lot about the company's products, they also understand their social environment very well. The number of successful co-creation stories keeps growing by the day. Relying heavily on web-based technology, particularly Web 2.0, the technical possibilities for bringing together a large group of people to develop a co-creation platform have increased considerably. If companies are using these strategies and aim at using their superpromoters, their sales will have exponential growth potential. Remember, superpromoters not only have the right kind of knowledge of both product and their social context, they also are used to having influence and telling people their opinions. A superpromoter should take to the interaction going on at a co-creation platform like a fish to water; a great way for companies to save on their R&D expenses.

Cost saving # 4: Quality control

It never ceases to amaze me what a special internet-based phenomenon Wikipedia is: here you have an encyclopedia written entirely by volunteers. That's special, we all agree, but what makes it almost seem bizarre is that anyone can edit, change or add to it. Shouldn't Wikipedia be riddled with errors and mistakes? Experience has taught us that the opposite is true. It is more error-free than other encyclopedias! How on earth could that be? It is because contributors and users of Wikipedia are themselves the guardians of its content and quality. If someone tries to sabotage an entry by deliberately inserting wrong or misleading information, others will immediately – often within hours – correct this. People obviously feel involved with the Wiki-project to the extent that they are willing to volunteer their spare time to be quality controllers. That, in a nutshell, is what superpromoters do with the products and services they care about! All communication tools at their disposal will be deployed to correct a wrong, and if they were to have access to Wiki-tools, they'd be repairing the product they care so much about, themselves, as well. The budget item "Quality Control" has just shrunk…

Cost saving # 5: Reduced staff turnover
We have talked before about ways in which superpromoters can also motivate the people working for "their" company. And we all know that motivated staff is more productive and more client oriented than their unmotivated brethren. There is an indirect effect on a company's finances as a consequence, but we can safely predict a direct effect in terms of lowered staff turnover figures. Regular exposure to a superpromoter is clearly enough to keep people happy in their jobs…at least, happy enough not to be looking for another one.

How to Create, Nurture and Assist your Superpromoters

The fundamental premise of *The Superpromoters* is that businesses that manage to create and nurture their superpromoters will have the largest sales figures and the best reputation. In Chapter 5, we will investigate ways in which to encourage a superpromoter's enthusiasm, how influencing works and can be supported. The basic reason why enthusiastic customers are created is because a business manages to create something for which there is demand. Being able to supply the goods is the *sine qua non* for that enthusiasm. But the subsequent manner of dealing with customers will often be the seeding of future superpromoters. You do this, for example, by being able to offer a customer a pleasant surprise, such as exceeding their expectations, showing them how much you appreciate their custom, or going all-out to help them with something troublesome. It is during these moments that superpromoters are born...sometimes even for life! My personal example of this sort of thing happened a few years ago after my home had been burgled. The thieves had taken a new leather coat, a videorecorder and a wad of foreign banknotes, for which I obviously didn't have a receipt. In fact, I was even wondering whether I would bother mentioning it to the insurance company, Interpolis. So, when I called them and happened to mention it anyway, you can imagine how surprised I was when they were not at all fussed by my lack of receipts for the foreign cash and told me to just add it to my claim. They were saying that they trusted me! No surprise then, that I became really enthusiastic about Interpolis. A burglary is a very emotionally disturbing experience for most of us; therefore, if your insurer is really there for you, offering support and trusting you, this will help to form a most positive experience. Interpolis employees have confirmed that they have managed to create quite a number of enthusiastic clients by acting in this manner. My experience with another insurance company was that I felt as if I were the potential criminal, not the victim, when I tried to make a claim. Their entire focus was on preventing fraud. But I have learned you can also do business another way!

So, any business that is aiming to create superpromoters had better be on their toes during those times they're in direct contact with their customers, particularly during those moments when emotions could be running higher than normal. A typical example of this might occur when a complaint is made.

A complaint is a gift!

This may sound contradictory, but receiving a complaint is like getting a present. When a customer has been disappointed but they don't show you they are unhappy in any way, shape or form, there is nothing you can do about it. For all you know, they might just go over to your competitor and you'll never hear from them again. But it is likely that they will be telling their immediate environment all about their experience, which means that your damage is potentially far greater than merely losing one customer. The point is that getting a complaint is an opportunity to strengthen your relationship with your customer...provided it is handled properly, of course.

There is a negative emotion at work the moment a customer makes a complaint. They have been disappointed, and, who knows, even experienced all kinds of problems because something related to your product or service did not go as it should have. Not being available or not providing an adequate response can be a most frustrating experience for your customer at such times. This is how antipromoters are made! But handling complaints properly should not only be about limiting the number of potential antipromoters, because if, at those times, you manage to deal with a complaint with respect and understanding, you don't just appease a customer, you might be assisting at the birth of a superpromoter!

Combating antipromoters

We are all agreed. The best way of avoiding antipromoters is to offer good service and to treat your customers with respect. That is why we keep making the point in *The Superpromoter* to stick with your superpromoters and follow what they do. When they are being enthusiastic about you there's nothing to worry about. Just keep on making them happy and try to involve them with your ideas. But, if they start to grumble, things take on an entirely different dimension. That's when you have to pay close attention; you are not going to be making antipromoters if you are able to convey that you truly appreciate their opinions, and are sincerely doing everything you can to arrive at a solution.

Well, we all know that in real life we all make mistakes now and then. If that has happened to you and you've made some antipromoters as a result, try to track them down. Larger companies can easily read online what's being said about them. This means that when you have tracked down your antipromoter you have another opportunity to listen to them and show them that you are willing to try and repair the relationship. If businesses respond well there is an opportunity of yet converting the unhappy antipromoter.

Ma Bell cancels bill of famous Twitterer

AMSTERDAM – Adam Savage, TV Presenter of a popular show called Mythbusters was recently sent a staggering US$11,000 bill for using his mobile phone to surf online while he was abroad. When he complained about this "rip-off" on Twitter his bill was canceled by AT&T.

The story is that Adam had made use of a mobile USB-Modem to surf the web while he was in Canada. According to AT&T he had received 9 gigabytes of data doing this. The US, like all other countries, has very steep charges for mobile internet use across borders. Savage ventilated his anger about his phone bill on Twitter, calling on tens of thousands of fans to spread his message around. The microbloggers had soon propelled "AT&T" up the ladder to become one of the most popular subjects that day, which otherwise was mainly abuzz with comments on the death of Michael Jackson.

Savage Attention

That same day AT&T reached the angry TV star by phone and his phone bill was ripped up. "You clearly have enough followers on Twitter to capture our attention," said Ma Bell's employee, quite openly.

KLM

A growing number of companies are turning to services such as Twitter to keep an ear to the ground for what their customers are saying. A Dutch entrepreneur, Marc van der Chijs, recently found himself upgraded from Economy to Business Class after he had complained about KLM's service on Twitter.

Message found on nu.nl, July 6, 2009

When the antipromoters have distanced themselves from your business to the extent that they won't have anything to do with you anymore, you had better keep the same distance yourself. All that you can do effectively in those circumstances is to provide ammunition to your superpromoters for their battle against the antipromoters. They are the last man standing who can convert or disarm the antipromoter, in a last-ditch damage control operation.

The ultimate battle
Ultimately, a company's reputation and sales growth are being determined by the battle between superpromoters and

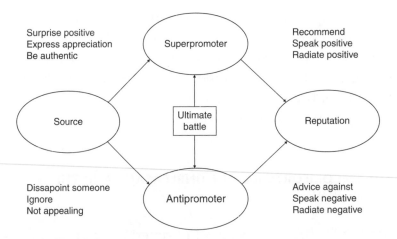

Figure 3.2 The ultimate battle

antipromoters. Superpromoters are fighting for you tooth and nail while antipromoters are ripping you to shreds. Less bloodthirsty, we can imagine the battle as a kind of debate between *pro* and *anti*. Who is most persuasive? Other customers are keeping an eye on both sides, ready to take their advice or copy their behavior. The side with the most followers determines the fate of the company. As the biggest stakeholder, the company should follow the arguments closely, keeping a close tally of the number of superpromoters versus the number of antipromoters. Equally important, you must be up to speed on what's being said by both sides. That is how superpromoters can be supported with information they can use during the debate, while antipromoters are silenced as their arguments are dismantled.

If you think ahead, the conclusions that will be drawn at the end of *The Superpromoter* are already becoming clear. Business should be focusing on their superpromoters and antipromoters. If they are able to create, nurture and manage superpromoters, and assist them while also managing to battle their antipromoters successfully, their success will grow. Not every company will be able to harness the energies of their superpromoters effectively, however. The reasons for this can be traced to things that are uncomfortable, unpleasant or unknown.

THE UNCOMFORTABLE, THE UNPLEASANT AND THE UNKNOWN

Aiming for the active support of superpromoters as a business strategy takes guts. If you are not prepared to abandon the safe and familiar world of conventional mass-media advertising campaigns and product development that is the result of Central Planning, you are going to face some tough moments. Don't say you weren't warned, but what follows may frighten some people...

The uncomfortable

So far it all seems so simple. From now on you let your marketing be done by your superpromoters and hey presto! All done! Sorry, it's not really that simple. The problem is that it can be very uncomfortable. You are going to be ceding control to a group of people who aren't even on the payroll and won't be managed directly by you. They are not going to let you push them around; they are doing what they're doing because they are sincerely enthusiastic about your company or your product, and because this is the way things are done according to their social mores. They are not doing it because they are seeking gain (except possibly a gain in social status), or because they want the shareholders to make more money. And they are not doing it for their bosses, colleagues or to improve things at work. Instead, they are doing it for personal reasons; their personal involvement and enthusiasm and because they believe their social circle will also care to know. The superpromoter's motivation therefore is both intrinsic and social. Not only are they a critical breed, but they also expect that people are going to listen to them, so, making use of their qualities and influence does not come without a price tag. If this rather delicate process is not managed well, superpromoters can turn into antipromoters and may cause a lot of damage. In aiming for the superpromoter you'll have to be prepared to give up a good amount of control... and make sure that you take the superpromoter very seriously. At times this might feel uncomfortable.

The unpleasant

Since we've just concluded that you cannot have any direct control over your superpromoters, a logical consequence of that conclusion is that superpromoters can also display undesirable behavior... be unpleasant, in short.

Some superpromoters might be dyed-in-the-wool conservatives, for example, which could be unpleasant if you are trying to do something innovative. Loyal visitors of Center Parcs holiday villages don't want anything to change! They like it just the way it is. They feel proprietary about "their" place and will argue to keep it "pristine". Many businesses, especially the ones that have been around for longer, have this kind of customer. They are the customers who became enthusiastic years ago and like nothing better than to have their (original) positive experience be repeated over and over. If market circumstances dictate change, it might, unfortunately, present a problem for both the company and the customer. And that makes it a difficult challenge to innovate in order to attract new business. This is a dilemma that needs to be resolved at the highest possible level, since making the wrong strategic choice has sounded the death knell for many a company. If the changes happen too quickly, or are too far-reaching for the taste of loyal super-promoters it may cause them to feel abandoned and turn against you. This produces unhappy results for the business, particularly if it has not yet reached the critical mass of new clients needed to ensure adequate substitute turnover. All of this has the potential of being, well, unpleasant.

Where there are loyal customers who neither expect nor desire any form of innovation, the superpromoters will be acting as guardians of the soul of the business. They represent a tough group to support you in making any changes, since their main fear is that you'll be selling your soul to the devil. The challenge in these situations is therefore clear: how to make the required changes in a creative way that preserves the company's soul. Fortunately, superpromoters would be more than happy to sit down with you and figure this out. They appreciate being taken seriously, and there is a good chance they might be able to dream up solutions that nobody in the company could have come up with. In these circumstances it is a smart idea to seek the advice of both conservative (old) and potential (new) superpromoters in a discussion on innovation...and then follow it. By working together with both groups of superpromoters a way can be found to keep the conservatives enthusiastic while making the necessary changes. This approach, designed to avoid their feeling neglected, has the most chance of generating practical suggestions from them. Provided they support the change, they will also be able to explain the need for change to their – probably equally conservative – environment.

The unknown

There are many companies that do not actually believe they have superpromoters. They are unknown to them. For example, insurance companies, or electric utility companies, find it hard to believe they have customers who could be enthusiastic about their services. It is unquestionably true that they will have fewer superpromoters than the likes of Dell, BMW or IKEA, but there is equally no doubt that you could track down several enthusiasts. Like the person who was really helped out by their insurers, or someone who was pleasantly surprised by some top quality service from the utility repairmen. These types of companies will also have superpromoters working for them and, in any event, will have employees capable of creating new superpromoters – even if their bosses are not aware of this. If they've been listening to dissatisfied customers these bosses will definitely know what they're doing wrong. However, as we've said before, this renders the superpromoter invisible to the company, and out of sight means out of mind... and unloved. After all, it's bad enough to lose control of the management of your company; losing it to the great unknown must be worse.

IN CONCLUSION... AND PEEKING FORWARD

We have just been discovering that it can be scary and a nuisance to be aiming for the collaboration of superpromoters.

But it is even scarier not to be aiming for superpromoters. They exist with or without your blessing; regardless of whether you are aiming for them or not they will be doing their thing anyway...and that surely applies to their alter ego, the antipromoter. This is why businesses and other organizations would be better served risking a hop, skip and a jump to the third step of the evolution immediately. You do not distinguish yourself with your excellence by merely aiming for customer satisfaction, something many companies seek to do with their quality control systems and consumer satisfaction research. Aiming for enthusiasm, the second step in the evolution, is a step in the right direction, but in the end it is the customer who influences the world around them with their enthusiasm, who determines a company's reputation, and even their sales growth! These are the people to get to know, to combine forces with. May the force...!

The next chapter will start to assemble the toolbox required to identify your superpromoters and antipromoters. We will be discussing how you can measure enthusiasm, and the sharing of enthusiasm and influence.

4

THE TOOLBOX

Having now met and spent some time getting to know our superpromoter, we've had a chance to learn a bit more about their role in the evolution of customer orientation. Time to take a look in this chapter at the toolbox we'll need to work with superpromoters. We will in particular be focusing on the measurement criteria (the metrics) required to identify superpromoters and to keep track of them.

Let us return for a moment to our definition of superpromoter:

A superpromoter is an enthusiast who shares and wears their enthusiasm, and influences other people by spreading it around.

Superpromoters have to meet three criteria:

1. They must be enthusiastic.
2. Their enthusiasm must be shared with others.
3. The enthusiast must have influence over others.

Given that there are three elemental criteria to meet before anybody can be called a superpromoter, this gives us three metrics with which to measure our definition:

1. **EM** (Enthusiasm Metric)
2. **SSM** (Social Sharing Metric)
3. **IFM** (Influence Metric)

These definitional metrics, although a bit clunky, have international currency and are therefore recognizable to many. This avoids confusion.

Let us begin by looking inside our toolbox for the right one for determining EM, the Enthusiasm Metric. The first tool we'll need is the *Net Promoter Score®*[25], which allows us to measure enthusiasm. The reason we're using NPS® in *The Superpromoter* is simple: companies around the globe are now implementing this methodology, which also happens to fit seamlessly onto the theoretical framework we are developing here. It offers companies an excellent basis for identifying their superpromoters and only requires minor modification to be used for finding them as well. The NPS®-methodology is not necessarily the only tool you'll need in order to work with a superpromoter strategy; there are also alternative measurements for enthusiasm. Depending on individual circumstances, several other EMs may be more suited. Once we have discussed the NPS® we'll return to alternative EMs for a further look.

THE NET PROMOTER SCORE® (NPS®) AS MEASUREMENT FOR ENTHUSIASM

The fact that the world at large has come to appreciate the importance of customers' willingness to promote a company to other potential customers (aka *word of mouth* and *consumer advocacy*) is largely due to imaginative work by Frederick F. Reichheld, partner at Bain & Company. His 2003 article in the *Harvard Business Review*[26] showed that the best predictor of sales growth could basically be captured by the research question, "How likely is it that you would recommend company X to a friend or colleague?" Discovering the correlation between consumer advocacy and growth in turnover was a major step forward in the development of a superpromoter theory. The survey being described by Reichheld involved thousands of customers of more than four hundred businesses spread across six separate industries. It was Reichheld's aim to discover which dimension of customer relationships would be the best predictor of a company's top-line growth. Prior to the article's publication in HBR, Reichheld had already developed quite a reputation as a "Loyalty-Guru", having written such best-sellers as *The Loyalty Effect* (1996)[27] and *Loyalty Rules* (2001)[28]. Considering his interest in loyalty, it wasn't a great surprise to learn that he anticipated a loyalty-related question to be his best predictor. Unfortunately, neither loyalty, nor satisfaction returned any significant causative correlation with top-line growth. Originally intended only as a question to measure a customer's willingness to recommend, the one that demonstrated a positive correlation was:

> *"How likely is it that you would recommend company X to a friend or colleague?"*

This question offered the best correlation with turnover growth statistics for the four hundred companies in the survey. In the same article, Reichheld described a new metric he developed together with Satmetrix with which

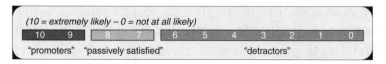

Figure 4.1 Deriving the NPS®

to measure a customer's willingness to recommend and called it the Net Promoter Score (NPS®). NPS® is derived as follows:

The question on willingness to recommend can be graded on the scale as shown in Figure 4.1.

The proportion of customers answering the question above with a 9 or 10 score (on a 1 – 10 scale) is called **promoters**. Those customers grading it 6 or lower are **detractors**, while those grading it with an 8 or 7 score are called passively satisfied, or **passives**. The Net Promoter Score® is then derived by subtracting the percentage of detractors from the percentage of promoters.

Assume that 40% of customers score a 9 or 10, and 10% grade the question with a 6 or lower; the NPS® score will then be 30% (40% minus 10%).

Calculating NPS® is therefore captured in the following formula:

NPS® = % promoters minus % detractors

Not all detractors are antipromoters

Detractors are not necessarily also antipromoters. A detractor is a customer who indicates that his willingness to recommend the company is low. But that does not go as far as saying that he will discourage others, or even has the intention to discourage. A detractor could just as easily be indifferent about the company, whereas an antipromoter has a decidedly negative image, and makes no bones about it! They do tell others not to use the company or its products. Antipromoters, as we discussed earlier, are also influencers; detractors don't necessarily fall into that category at all.

The NPS® represents a strict measure of a customer's willingness to engage in word-of-mouth recommendation. Only those who have indicated a top score (that it is "very likely" that they will be making a recommendation [grade 9 or 10]), make a positive contribution to the score, while those responding to the question with a 6 or lower cause the score to go down. Note that grade 7 or 8 are considered to be indifferent, and are not included in the score, in either a positive or negative sense. The implication of this scoring system is that only the companies with high NPS®-scores are those where the vast majority of customers are very enthusiastic about the product or service on offer.

Using NPS® as a measure of customer appreciation has grown in importance among many industries. Large international companies such as Philips Electronics, General Electric and Lego consider the NPS® to be one of the most important performance indicators to determine how they are running their business. Why is NPS® this popular? Time for us to delve a bit deeper into this puzzle, and consider its pros and cons carefully.

The success of NPS®

Reichheld managed to get customer surveys on the agenda of the boards of many big businesses. The list of CEOs of multinational companies around the world who have had Reichheld's writings on their bedside table is large and still growing. How did he manage this? Let's make a summary of the most important reasons:

NPS® is relatively easy

Anybody who is running a sophisticated organization is always on the lookout for ways of simplifying complex realities. Unfortunately for them, the average research report resulting from consumer surveys is not very simple to digest, and in most cases is surely not inspirational. These reports (we've all seen them) are loaded with tables, graphs and sterile analysis; enough to make even the researchers who prepared them feel uninspired. Imagine what it is doing at board level! Research firms have a habit of coming up with complicated models that are intended to present the results of their customer surveys clearly. Clearly? Well, not always quite…Every research agency has developed its own ways of modeling, which is hard to compare, from firm to firm, but also from model to model. More often than not, this level of complexity is lost at the top of the organization, where it accordingly does not get the attention it might deserve. Management tend to look for that one and simple measure. They want to put the measure together with other important key performance indicators (KPI) on their dashboard and keep driving. Prior to the arrival of NPS® the KPI used to measure customer satisfaction was usually based on a composite index.

Many businesses make use of "customer barometers" that have been made up of an index composed of a dozen or so measurements. These might cover such things as satisfaction with the account manager, or with the price/quality relationship, and so on. Each factor being measured is then also given its own weighting within the index; making it possible, for example, that being satisfied with the helpdesk counts for twice as much as being satisfied with delivery speed. Perhaps this weighting was created because customers actually feel it to be twice as important, but it could equally be included because the company's management considers some measurements to be of the greater strategic importance.

One can make a rational argument in defense of such a composite "barometer". The index combines everything that is important, and everything that is important has been given a weighting to rank its relative placement in the index. The advantage of using an index put together in this way is that different indicators, such as satisfaction, covering several aspects of the subject being measured can now be

3 Satisfaction aspects		4 Satisfaction score		5 Weight		6 Score x weight	
7	Proposal stage	8	7	9	0,15	10	1,05
11	Account management	12	8	13	0,52	14	4,16
15	Products/services	16	7	17	0,41	18	2,87
19	Price/Quality	20	7	21	0,45	22	3,15
23	Order	24	6	25	0,11	26	0,66
27	Delivery	28	7	29	0,09	30	0,63
31	Information provider	32	8	33	0,30	34	2,40
35	Customer service	36	5	37	0,22	38	1,10
39	Invoicing	40	7	41	0,08	42	0,56
43	Dealing with complaints	44	6	45	0,23	46	1,38
47	**Height of the barometer**					48	**1,80**

Table 4.1   Example of a customer barometer

studied through one single number. The problem, however, is that it has become harder to understand what that one figure actually represents. Using a single measurement therefore complicates matters for management or staff who have to work with the results of the survey. Because the subtleties are not present, there is a risk that the focus could dissipate.

In comparison with an index as just described it is less complicated to use a performance indicator, such as the NPS®, based on one single question; this is much simpler and easier to understand. In conclusion, we can say that complex models provoke resistance and do not release much creative energy. In fact, reading this section serves as an admirable example of just what we're talking about! NPS® is already a simplification, but only counting the number of promoters without subtracting the detractors simplifies this KPI even further. It will be the only number you'll need to identify your superpromoters.

NPS® is related to top-line growth

A company's management needs straightforward measurements that make meaningful statements about how their business is performing. Such measurements must necessarily include hard financial indicators such as sales and profits. Nowadays they also tend to include softer measurements such as customer and employee satisfaction, for the company to factor into their thinking. A steadily growing number of companies are exchanging their customer-satisfaction scorecards for NPS®, because it holds the promise of being a better predictor of company-sales growth. This being the one thing that most companies want to predict, naturally! It is probably fair to say that, provided a demonstrable relationship between the two can be established, this indicator is more valuable than financial indicators. The latter can only tell us something about what has happened in the past, while indicators such as the NPS® can tell us something about future growth trends. No wonder that private equity outfits have been showing a greater interest in "soft" indicators such as customer loyalty. Since Private Equity is in the business of spending money on bets on the future when buying companies, they are obviously much keener to find out about what will happen than to learn about what has happened. For private equity as much as for the rest of us, it is essential to have a good understanding of the relationship between NPS® and top-line growth within a given industry.[29] Everything you have been reading about NPS® notwithstanding, not many companies have been able to "prove" the existence of a strong relationship between their NPS®-score and growing sales figures. The secret of the NPS® appears also to be based on a company's managers believing in the theory. The implicit promise that it correlates with growth, combined with the logic of how enthusiastic customers bringing in new customers producing growth, will be sufficient for many businesses to implement the NPS® methodology, no further questions asked. A little further along in this chapter we will see that the proportion of superpromoters exhibits an equally solid correlation with a company's top-line growth as the NPS®.

NPS® and Net Promoter Score® are copyrighted terms, not to be used without attribution

We should point out, however, that the terms NPS® and Net Promoter Score are both subject to copyright restrictions, which means they cannot be used without attribution. The Superpromoter has therefore consistently been adding a little trademark logo to the term. The owners of the NPS® en Net Promoter Score brand names, Bain, Reichheld & Satmetrix, will threaten will legal action anyone using the material without its copyright designation, whether in print or advertising. You are free, however, to use the underlying issue, which looks at willingness to make recommendations, that after all, was being used by other research firms long before Reichheld developed its use in his survey. So, pay attention when using the terms NPS® and Net Promoter Score®.

NPS® is a sensitive and stimulating measurement

A disadvantage of scoring satisfaction on a 1–10 scale is that generally speaking the results tend to gravitate toward the 6–7.5 range. A probably unintended consequence of this phenomenon is that interest in customer-satisfaction surveys tends to wane after a few measurements, both for companies and research agencies. It is hard to remain motivated when not much is happening. When a grade of 7.2 drifts down to 7.1 the desire to leap into the breach is easily suppressed. An NPS® measurement, on the other hand, is much more volatile than a "regular" satisfaction scorecard. The NPS® might show an extreme range from +100 to –100, while in actual practice a scoring range from –50 to +50 is a common occurrence. So, when the results of an NPS® measurement register movements of 10 or even 20 points, this shift will be the cause of great discussion... but at least these results are getting attention, and the willingness to do something is far greater than when the movement was measured in basispoints.

Another advantage is that the sensitivity of the NPS® causes disruptions – or better, subtle shifts, in customer relations – to now be picked up that much earlier. It is a much more sensitive antenna in comparison. Clearly, this heightened sensitivity can partially be explained by the calculation method used. By calibrating the NPS® to exclude respondents with less extreme opinions, the measure becomes more "extreme". The seriously enthusiastic promoters and the critical detractors are determining the final results. The – often – larger group of customers who think it's all OK or so-so, are filtered out of the equation. But sensitivity cannot be entirely explained away by mathematical considerations. The willingness to make word-of-mouth recommendations has a strong emotional component. Word of mouth can only develop if there exists a strong and positive connection with the product, brand or service. This type of emotional connection will exhibit greater volatility than more stable, rational, considerations.

Weaknesses of the NPS®

Some of the strong points of the NPS® we have just been discussing are also its weaknesses. Let's take a closer look.

Disturbances and undesirable disruptions
The fact that the NPS® is more volatile than other forms of satisfaction-measurement keeps an organization on its toes. Having said that, if the volatility cannot be explained adequately, or if employees cannot be given clear guidance on what is expected of them, this might be disturbing. This concern is even more relevant if the NPS® is being used for employee evaluations or as a tool for establishing

bonus targets. While the NPS® dynamics are still unclear, it is surely sensible to exercise great caution in using it to evaluate your people, or to decide how much money they will earn.

This super antenna, the sensitive NPS® method, is not an unqualified advantage. Yes, there is an advantage in disturbances in customer relationships being picked up earlier, but it is picking up more static as well. From experience I can add that undesirable disruptions due to measurement methods are just the type of thing that keeps market researchers awake at night. The fact that the NPS® is super sensitive also makes it vulnerable to measuring error; even measuring things at different times of day can have an effect on the results. Otherwise it could perhaps be the big football match, a hot day, or summer holidays; all known examples of the things that influence a survey. The more sensitive the measuring instrument, the greater the potential trouble. Only with fairly constant conditions will the effects be kept reasonably under control. Something to keep in mind.

Cultural sensitivities of the NPS®
The NPS® is very sensitive to differences in culture. Its scores are highest in Latin America and lowest in Asia, an important thing to factor into the equation if you are a multinational organization. You cannot take your Japanese manager to task for the fact that his scores are consistently lower than those of his Brazilian counterpart. One advantage of implementing an NPS® worldwide is that we are better able to identify international differences due to cultural sensitivities, and therefore can also provide a better interpretation. A good rule of thumb in North America, for

example, is that an NPS® of 25 or higher[30] represents quite a good score. In Europe a score greater than 10 is considered very decent; Americans and Canadians, however, tend to express themselves somewhat more forcefully. As a matter of fact, this may lead to both very high and very low scores. The NPS® has been designed in a manner that high scores (9 or 10) will have a higher impact on the overall scoring, whereas a very low score (1 or 2) has the same effect as a 6. The implication of this is that in Europe, where 9 or 10 scores are still rare and unusual (giving an 8 is considered pretty adventurous), the NPS® tends towards lower numbers. There has been some debate on resetting the European grading scale, so that a 0 – 5 grade is considered a detractor and an 8 – 10 grade a promoter. This makes sense from the point of view that it reflects the European approach and usage of the grading system; it 'feels' fair to them. Someone who gives a score of 8 in Europe is likely to be someone who will recommend by word of mouth. Yet, according to Reichheld, there is an observable difference between people who give 9 – 10 scores and those who give an 8, with the former giving recommendations significantly more often than the latter. Analysis indicates that in the Netherlands for example, this turning point averages one full grade point lower. There, people likely to recommend give scores of 8 or higher; those with only a willingness to recommend at a score of 7 or lower are significantly less likely to actually make recommendations. Nearly all companies who share their insights during international NPS® conferences[31] on the implementation of a global NPS® methodology, stress the importance of identifying benchmarks for individual countries. Cultural differences can be so great that cross border comparisons are of little use. Better to compare a company's NPS® within a country's borders and in the context of its local competitors. This is also true for other EMs or satisfaction scorecards. Since other indicators also tend to have issues relating to cultural sensitivities, the search for a local benchmark is always the wiser option.

The NPS® is not always a good measure of enthusiasm

An important problem for the NPS® is that it does not always measure what it says it measures. This is because a recommendation is not always related to actual enthusiasm for the product. The situations where this is the case were described near the end of section "Evolutionary Step # 2: Aiming for Enthusiasm". Scarcity was one possible cause mentioned, and that is something which could lead to misleading measurements from the NPS®. The following example will illustrate why a low NPS® does not have to be bad news for a company like eBay. Because hundreds of thousands of people are in the business of offering their wares on eBay, the online auctioneer has for several years now been one of the largest job creators in the world. Although they are not employed by eBay, it does provide its users with either a secondary source of income or/and often even a primary source, all based on their online business volume.

A remarkable new survey by A.C. Nielsen International Research finds that about 724,000 Americans use eBay – online auctioneer and general marketplace – for their primary or secondary income. That figure is up from about 430,000 Americans in a similar 2004 survey. In other words, about 300,000 people have started businesses on eBay in the past year. So eBay can properly be viewed as America's No. 1 generator of, not just businesses, but jobs.

As David Faber of CNBC said recently, "If eBay employed the…people who earn an income selling on its site, it would be the nation's No. 2 private employer, behind Wal-Mart."

Source: www.inyourweb.com, date Tuesday, August 30, 2005

Someone who is earning a large part of his income by selling comic books on eBay will undoubtedly be enthusiastic about the possibilities that have opened up for them online. Yet, they are unlikely to score highly with respect to their willingness to recommend. The problem, of course, is that these entrepreneurs have absolutely no intention of giving others the idea to start doing the same thing. They are making – hopefully – a tidy pot of money because they have found a niche where they can ply their trade. Often, it will involve a highly specialized form of merchandise (like post-1987 Manga comics, or pre-WW II Action Comics.) that only appeals to a very small clientele. The World Wide Web makes it feasible to find and market to these groups.[32] Buyer and seller find each other via eBay and create a marketplace large enough to be viable. Having "cornered" a piece of the market, the last thing you are going to do is tell others to come and exploit it as well. It is easy to set up a business online, but it can also be copied very easily. Who wants to create their own competition? As your little business is turning a nice trade, the more people become interested the less you'll be inclined to advertise that fact. That's the reason why those who are most enthusiastic about doing business online through eBay will produce the lowest NPS®.

During an NPS® conference the speaker from eBay told the audience that they had found a pragmatic solution to keeping alive the enthusiasm of eBay's top management for NPS®, notwithstanding the fact that it isn't a very good indicator of enthusiasm and shows negative correlation with sales growth. The solution is that they were able to come up with another question that is a good indicator for their top-line performance. That question is:

> *"Do you think you'll still be trading through eBay in three years time?"*

This question is very different from the one asking about willingness to make a recommendation, and furthermore, is measured on a 1 – 5 scale. The eBay people still call it their NPS® question though! They have made it possible for top managers to obtain an NPS® and also made sure that the score has been based on the correct EM. Not only a very pragmatic solution in my opinion, but it also offers the advantage that NPS® enthusiasm is maintained without another KPI getting too much attention. Sometimes, or so they seem to think at eBay, the best solution is the one that works!

Another difficulty in interpreting the NPS® is that a customer may either recommend a product or service, or do exactly the opposite. Which it will be depends on the person the customer intends to be the recipient of his recommendation. A large customer of one of the big accounting firms, for example, indicated that he would recommend his accountants to the CEO of another large firm, but not to his cousin, who is a butcher. The butchers', if for no other reason than the expense involved, would be far better off with a local accounting firm. We could also find several examples involving consumer products. One example would be the latest mobile phone with all the trimmings: you might recommend it to your brother, but definitely not to your grandmother. In fact, there are several underlying factors that can complicate your interpretation of an NPS®. Take a low NPS® for example: it doesn't automatically mean that buying the product in question is being discouraged. It might just mean that someone is not very interested in this product, or suspects that their social circle is not. The NPS® is therefore unsuitable for identifying antipromoters, unless you make an assumption that most antipromoters are to be found among customers scoring a 3, or lower. We will elaborate on this in the following paragraph. However, this group will most certainly also include other customers, whose statement that they will not recommend is only based on their expectation that their social network isn't interested in the product. None of these scenarios leading to a lower NPS® are really about lack of enthusiasm for the product itself, at least not the customer's; here the lack of interest stems from their social environment.

The NPS® is more complicated than necessary
In comparison with the highly complex indexes used by some companies to gain a sense of their customers' levels of appreciation, the NPS® is relatively uncomplicated. Nevertheless, the scorecard used is more complex than it actually needs to be. The only number that says something about enthusiastic customers is the number of promoters. The other side, detractors, is not that interesting for our purposes, since it includes people who might be indifferent or choose not to recommend for other reasons. The only

ones we care about among detractors are the antipromoters. The research done by Otker et al.[33] demonstrates that those customers giving scores of 3 or lower have a willingness to discourage others. The entire group of detractors is therefore too disparate for us to take into account. In any case, the NPS® can only give you an indication about antipromoters; identifying them requires another approach. Remember, if customers are disinclined to make recommendations, this does not necessarily mean they are downright negative, either. The metrics for identifying your antipromoters described in section "Identifying the Antipromoter" are more suitable.

A survey conducted by *Blauw Research* in collaboration with Erasmus University Rotterdam, modeled on Reichheld's earlier research, also identified a correlation between the NPS® and the financial results measured for the period 2002 – 2008 of some 140 companies in the Netherlands.[34] Measuring the financial results against the isolated group of "promoters" offers a similar correlation, and from that we may conclude that "promoters" are equally as valid a performance indicator as the NPS®. The important point of difference is that this statistic is much easier to grasp than a composite score such as NPS®.

The expectation exists that the proportion of superpromoters and antipromoters will demonstrate an even stronger correlation to financial results, which would make them superior predictors. At this stage, however, superpromoters have not yet been part of survey metrics for long enough to constitute solid proof. Happily, early indications do point in that direction.

If we assume for the moment that detractors are not that relevant for our purposes, their continued influence on an important performance indicator can only be seen as a disturbance. Therefore, using promoters as "a star to steer her by" is a much better proposition. Those companies that have taken a third step down the evolutionary path could go one step further and steer their business course by the percentage of superpromoters and the percentage of antipromoters.

A trap to be avoided when implementing
the NPS® methodology: lack of focus on enthusiasm
Companies that have implemented the NPS® methodology seem well underway in steering their strategy in the direction of enthusiasm. However, the NPS® method is often applied in the same manner as customer-satisfaction surveys; the search is for things that need improving. Detractors get most attention since they appear to be the most dissatisfied. But that isn't necessarily the case, because the group also includes indifferent customers. For our purposes, customers who do not feel involved with either company or product, and therefore have no willingness to recommend, are not very interesting. After detractors, the next group receiving a lot of attention is the passives (scores of 7 or 8). If your purpose in using the NPS® methodology is to make promoters out of passives and detractors, then your, perhaps unintended, consequence is that the most enthusiastic customers – again – are getting the least attention. That is what happens if you think that you've achieved your goal in turning a customer into a promoter. Furthermore, because the question posed by the NPS® is usually included as an additional one in satisfaction surveys (most satisfaction surveys already included a question on willingness to recommend long before the NPS® had

made its appearance; the only thing is that in those days it wasn't given enough attention), the natural inclination is to attempt to use satisfaction criteria to explain a willingness to recommend. Satisfaction surveys customarily explain general satisfaction levels from the perspective of underlying satisfaction criteria. It can usually be explained fairly well from its underlying criteria (see Figure 4.2).

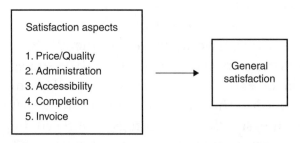

Figure 4.2   Factors that influence overall satisfaction measurements

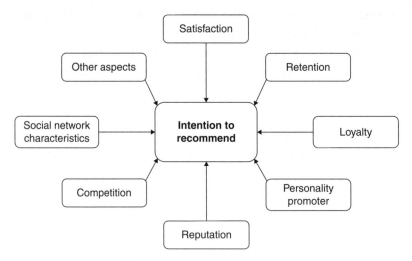

Figure 4.3   Factors that influence the intention to recommend

Willingness to make recommendations represents a different dimension altogether, and is also influenced by other factors. If a business wants to focus strategically on NPS® methods or for enthusiasm, other criteria must be factored into the model (see Figure 4.3).

One number is not enough for strategically focused management

When the NPS® has been implemented in its pure form, it is harder to recapture the underlying factors that have caused an increase or decrease of the NPS®. "Implementing in its pure form" as just used here means basing your measurements only on that question. That one question then corresponds with the "One Number" from the title of the 2003 article by Reichheld, *The One Number You Need to Grow*[35]. The problem, regrettably, is that one number does not give any clues as to why a certain level of NPS® was reached; that is, what the factors lying behind it are. If you cannot clearly establish which underlying changes in customer relationships have made the number go up or down, it gets harder to plan for focused improvements. Applying the NPS® in this manner will systematically risk that the commitment on the shopfloor or among middle management declines fast. This will be particularly true if the adoption of an NPS® methodology has been combined with the implementation of a new reward system, or links employee evaluations to the NPS® number.

In any event, even when NPS® has not been indexed to a bonus scheme for employees, it is definitely not a good idea to measure client-appreciation (their appreciation of you) based on just one question. If all you are measuring is the NPS® you will never know what you are doing well and cannot target the things that need improving, because you're not sure what they are. This is how customer measurement overshoots the mark. Without knowing how or why you have earned a given NPS® or what you could do to influence the score, your measurement will be of little value.

That is why organizations that measure the NPS® in its pure form are thin on the ground. Even Reichheld suggests that it is a good idea to pose another open question after asking the NPS® one. A number of large multinational companies have adopted this idea: first the NPS® question, and then an open one. This is where the question about whether there is room for improvement is posed, or an open question format is used. The follow-up question could be formulated as follows:

"Could you indicate how Company X could further improve itself?"

By asking this open question in addition to the NPS® number, information is collected about the reasons for why the NPS® score was given. "Why did customers come to this conclusion?"

Nonetheless, asking only one follow-up question may only provide you with superficial information. When asking for potential areas of improvement, most of your answers will focus on things being "cheaper", "better" and "faster". If you ask respondents why they will not make recommendations, you'll get answers such as, "That's something I never do...", or "Don't know anyone else who uses this product". Not that these answers aren't valuable, they are, but often you'd like to dig a little deeper to see what type of hard improvements need to be made, and most importantly, to find out what has made them enthusiastic in the first place. If the choice has been made to ask only one or two follow-up questions, a suggestion from Reichheld is to make follow-up telephone calls to customers in order to question them more deeply about the reasons behind their judgment. Most companies, in this situation, decide to focus on calling detractors in particular. Yet, it would be a great pity if a group of promoters receive little or no attention as a result.

Otherwise customer surveys are still basically being done the old-fashioned way, even if parading under the banner of an NPS® survey. In this case the company is still stuck in the first phase of the evolution toward customer orientation and is largely aimed at finding things to do better, and to repair those dissatisfactions that have been unearthed.

Another question that emerges when the NPS® method has been adopted in such minimalist fashion is whether it is wise to ask the question about willingness to make recommendations upfront, when asking a customer to evaluate your services. It doesn't seem right to open with that question. If the first thing you do is ask about their intention to make recommendations about you to others, it might even make a respondent a little suspicious whether crass commercial motives are not dictating the game. "Shouldn't you first be asking whether I'm actually satisfied before asking if I'd be recommending you?", is what the customer is thinking, even if not said aloud. During an NPS® conference in London I posed this question to Reichheld himself. It was his suggestion that it is sometimes wiser to first ask an opening question about satisfaction. Reichheld is clearly very pragmatic about this stuff, which is a good thing in his favor. His mission is to make a contribution to companies worldwide who wish to pay more attention to customer orientation. His message is "Ask few questions and measure the willingness to recommend through the NPS®". This is a clear message that has met with a great deal of enthusiastic acceptance. Many companies have a greater customer orientation as a result.

Pros and Cons of the NPS® considered

Although the NPS® methodology has a number of disadvantages and certain aspects of its approach have met with well-founded criticism,[36] it would nevertheless be a pity not to take advantage of its broad support among senior company executives. It is only fair to say that the NPS® will often work well, or at least as well as any other measurement, as long as its limitations are kept in mind. Furthermore, composite index numbers of an increasingly complex nature are not a viable option. They may be able to explain a bit more from scientific viewpoint, but their complexity tends to scare off exactly those people who should be working with them. Without their support, no system devised to measure customer appreciation will ever be a success. Not that this means we should avoid looking critically at the NPS®, quite the opposite, in fact! The advisors and researchers working with a company in this area should be looking carefully at the objections and be fine-tuning whenever necessary. And of course they ought to have a good working knowledge of the NPS®, and be measuring more than just that criterion. Finally, their job is to assist a company's executives to translate insights gained into effective action taken. Not easy to do: you're working with complicated data, in a dynamic model. Yet, this is supposed to be the added value that advisors bring. In short, keep it simple for the people in charge by supporting a relatively simple metric that has worldwide support, while you, as advisor, must concentrate on all the details you are coping with in order to offer the best possible advice. It is always better to step into the third-class carriage of a train with wheels than the first-class one of a train without. Without the engine of management support pulling the train you'd never get out of the station anyway. If the NPS® method "ain't broke, don't fix it". Having said this, it is important not to fall into the same trap as can happen with a customer-satisfaction survey, when the result is that you go in search of things to improve. It is also a valuable idea to make room for superpromoters and antipromoters within your measurement framework. Small adjustment; big added value…

OTHER INDICATORS FOR ENTHUSIASM

Up to now we have been taking a long look at the NPS® and how it can be used and abused. Superpromoters, however, are not dependent on it. When used properly, the NPS® lets you know who your enthusiasts are in any case. Alternative measurements of enthusiasm can also be used to identify your enthusiasts and superpromoters. However, even if you ask an additional question to measure willingness to recommend, sometimes this willingness to recommend isn't a good indicator of enthusiasm at all. What follows are a number of alternative indicators with which to study enthusiasm.

Very satisfied

In previous chapters of *The Superpromoter* we have made several critical comments about traditional measurements that have customer-satisfaction metrics as their centerpiece. There are, however, a number of situations where asking a question on satisfaction might give a good measure of enthusiasm. Yet it then becomes important not to emphasize "average satisfaction", as is usually done in satisfaction surveys. Those surveys present a satisfaction number as an average score – of say 3.6 – on a 5-point scale. When used in this manner, a satisfaction score does not represent a measurement of enthusiasm, but merely a measure of that grey and unemotional thing called "average satisfaction". If, on the other hand, your focus is on the "very satisfied" group of customers, you will have created an indicator for enthusiasm. Any customer, who indicates that they are very satisfied, is expressing their enthusiasm almost by definition, merely from having added the word "very" to their statement of satisfaction. Our research suggests a strong connection between the category of promoters and the category of customers indicating they are "very satisfied". This also means that in many customer surveys the enthusiasts indicate both that they are "very satisfied" and that they are "very likely to recommend". Particularly in those situations where a question on willingness to recommend is not a good indicator of enthusiasm (see section "Evolutionary Step # 2: Aiming for Enthusiasm"), a suitable alternative can be created by focusing on very satisfied customers instead. In situations where the product or service is scarcely available, or when the market is monopolistic, a question on satisfaction is a superior enthusiasm metric (EM) than the NPS®.

Will definitely remain as customer

In some cases a question on loyalty or retention may also be a good measure of enthusiasm. Examples of questions that measure customer loyalty are:

"Do you think you'll still be a customer three years from now?"
"Do you expect to be buying this product again?"
"Does company X deserves your loyalty?"

Loyalty questions are not suitable for all situations; for example, if supply is controlled by a monopoly, asking about loyalty is obviously rather silly. So is asking someone whether they expect to be filing their tax returns with the tax collector again next year...what's the alternative?...Jail? In this case you can really only ask about customer satisfaction with the taxman's level of service.

For those products that offer very little in terms of involvement (such as insurance) the loyalty question also has limited application. Because people aren't involved, this also means they don't think about the product very much, if at all, and consequently they really have no idea what they'll be doing in the future. In deciding to make a switch to another supplier, other factors play a role for the consumer, and it is unlikely that at the time the loyalty question is asked during a survey they will have clarity on their future intentions. What factors are going to determine the move to another seller? What enticements is the seller going to offer? All of this is unpredictable today.

In some situations the loyalty question is just fine for measuring enthusiasm. This could be in situations involving scarcity of supply, for example. A few pages ago we made a comparison with the role of scarcity in a love affair. The question...

"Do you think you'll be with the same partner in three years' time?"

...is an interesting barometer of the level of enthusiasm about the affair today. But it does not mean this question is a good predictor of future behavior. It is highly unlikely that the question throws any light on the likelihood that a 20-year old man will still be with his girlfriend in three years' time. Someone very much in love will of course say, passionately, that he'll still be with her, in three years or forever. But...after three long years the first bloom of love will have faded and it will take more effort to keep the relationship going. But his current level of enthusiasm for his girlfriend does come shining through. The same scenario can apply to the products we buy. In conclusion, a loyalty question can be a useful indicator of the current level of enthusiasm, but it has little predictive value for future behavior.

Passive recommendation

There are certain products or services that we are less inclined to talk about in our everyday lives and therefore little enthusiasm is attached to them. In these situations it might be useful to pose the question in a more indirect manner. For example:

> *"If a friend or colleague were to ask you for advice, would you recommend product X?"*

This kind of question is more appropriate in this case as it contextualizes their cognitive thoughts with their social interaction. An additional advantage is that if consideration is being given to recommending a competitor instead, this is factored into the question. The standard question on recommending behavior allows respondents to make multiple recommendations for many different brands or products.

This will certainly be the case for low-involvement products. In financial services, for example, it is equally possible for the main relationship bankers to be recommended along with any other set of bankers. By asking this indirect question you're forcing your customers to make a choice and recommend the superior alternative.

SHARING ENTHUSIASMS; THE SOCIAL SHARING METRIC (SSM)

Having enthusiastic customers is a wonderful thing, and when they share their enthusiasm this makes it even more wonderful. The previous paragraph described how enthusiasm could be a rich but also complex dimension. Sharing enthusiasm is no less complex, and certainly no less rich. The structure and dynamics of a social network play an important role while the personalities of the transmitter and receiver of enthusiasm will also have influence over how it is shared. This may sound complicated, but it's really not difficult to work with an SSM. In order to measure whether enthusiasm is in fact being transferred by sharing, you will need a yardstick. Social Sharing Metrics are indicators of the measure of shared enthusiasm. Let's take a look at a couple of examples.

Actual recommendation

There is a straightforward way to discover if a willingness to recommend has actually translated into your customers making recommendations. You can ask them if they have made any recommendations over a preceding period.

In contrast with NPS®) that asks about intentions, this is a question about actual behavior. This is important because not every intention, or even willingness to make a recommendation, translates into an actual recommendation. Perhaps there has been no opportunity so far to make any recommendation, or perhaps the respondent overestimated their likely behavior. It is a lot more reliable to ask for factual observations of a person's own behavior than to ask about future intentions (even if your own!). When asked the question, most people will remember if they have made any recommendations in the recent past or not.

The fact that people make a recommendation to someone else is more than just a simple indication of their enthusiasm being expressed. It also tells you that the recommendation is something that fits with their social network, and obviously there are situations for more potential recommendations to be made. Someone with a great deal of enthusiasm for Oscar Peterson, the great jazz pianist, will not be able to share this enthusiasm if they have no friends or acquaintances who also care for jazz, or if they are never in the company of jazz fans, at clubs or concerts. Asking this question (whether somebody has made an actual recommendation) addresses this issue, and so becomes a useful SSM.

Talking with others

How much you talk positively with other people about a subject can also be considered an SSM. If you want to find out whether people are enthusiastic about a certain advertising video clip for example, it is useful to know if people are talking about it with each other and in what way. The more talk, the more likely it is that the ad campaign

142

is a success. This is true, even if the way people are talking about it turns out differently than was intended. Wrong talk is better than no talk at all.

Herd behavior

There is no doubt: enthusiasm is infectious. It can be shared, jumping from person to person, even without a word being spoken. People, as we know, have an almost irrepressible need to copy each other. When someone exudes enthusiasm for a certain product, others will, consciously or subconsciously, be intrigued to get a hold of one, too. Enthusiasm has many forms of expression, some even quite implicit. One is happy wearing a new outfit, the next wears his MP3-player with pride, or a third is visibly enjoying a new fruit drink. The urge to copy is even increased when it involves someone we consider our peer, or look up to.

Herd behavior, the urge to copy is not necessarily the immediate result of seeing somebody doing something that can be copied. Sometimes it is instantaneous; when someone orders a certain dish in a restaurant, the probability is relatively high that others at the table will order the same thing – as compared to the probability of them ordering any other dish on the menu. Waiters are hearing "I'm having what she's having" all the time. The herd is on the move…However, some types of copying may be postponed. The image of someone we observed drinking that new fruit drink with such visible delight has been stored in our memory, to come out and prompt us to put the same drink in our shopping cart at the supermarket three days later. We might not even notice why we did it. While we were doing something else, talking to someone over dinner, we observed, registered and filed it away. The influence it had comes out when the time is ripe, in this case in the soft drinks aisle.

There are some challenges in trying to use herd behavior as a measuring standard for enthusiasm. Part of the problem is that it largely plays out in our subconscious. This being the case, respondents in a survey are unable to tell us about behavior they are unaware of. There is also a cultural issue: Western civilization tends to frown on herd behavior. People appreciate (apparently[37]) original behavior. The implication of this cultural peculiarity is that, even if people are aware they are following a herd instinct, this does not mean that they are likely to admit it. Under ideal circumstances an independent observer would be able to verify copying behavior. Capturing people on hidden video camera in public places would allow observation of "natural" herd behavior taking place in the "wild", such as when people imitate each other's body language or posture. If you were to shadow a group of people for a certain amount of time, you will also learn who is copying whose enthusiasm. This would also be the way to bring your superpromoters to the surface. Unfortunately, this would be a highly costly and time-consuming exercise. There are also many laws and regulations governing privacy, thereby limiting what may or may not be done when filming people in public without their permission.

You can of course create certain "laboratory" experiments that allow you to observe specific herd behavioral aspects. If, for example, you place a group of people together and let them select among several different biscuits or soft drinks, there will be a proportion that copy the behavior of those who have already made their selection. For the researcher it can be very instructive to observe under which conditions herd behavior springs into action.

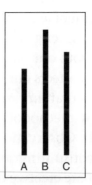

Figure 4.4   Asch's Card with lines

From experiments conducted by Solomon Asch[38] during the 1950s we can learn that people have a strong urge to yield to group pressures even when a stated group observation is perceived to be contrary to individually observed fact. In a nutshell, the Asch experiments went as follows: A group of participants to the experiment are shown a card with 2 or 3 lines, each of a distinctly different length.

When the individuals were asked to determine which line was the longest, nobody ever made a mistake. There was no doubt than line C is longer than line A, and that line B is longer than line C. In the experiment, however, all of the participants but one are a confederate of the experimenter, and have all been instructed to give a wrong answer. The real subjects believed however that the confederates were giving a serious answer. Then the real subjects were asked to determine which line was longest. A large number of them followed the majority and gave the wrong answer. Peer pressure is clearly such a powerful force that people will adjust their opinions just to belong. During interviews with real subjects of the Asch experiments afterward, they did confirm they had felt group pressure very clearly, that this confused them and that they adjusted their judgment as a result. Some even indicated that their perception of the length of the line was affected by peer pressure. Pressure from our peer groups not only affects our judgment, but it also affects our perceptions!

Business does not often attempt to measure herd behavior, in part because new methodologies would be required to conduct the research. Observation, although an obvious option, is both time-consuming and expensive. Another option would be to prepare creative questionnaires that take into consideration the implicit and subconscious nature of "infection by the herd". Let's say, for example, you want to know more about the role of copycat behavior among schoolchildren and how this affects their choice of chewing gum brand. The superpromoters would be the cool kids who are enthusiastic about a particular gum and share it unasked with their friends. We then can ask these kids if others are copying their choice of gum. By performing a number of measurements you can develop an understanding of how these processes unfold and what role superpromoters play in them. Basically, this means we are asking the superpromoters to observe their environment for us...letting them join our research team!

DETERMINING INFLUENCE;
THE INFLUENCE METRIC (IFM)

I hope that the discussion so far has described how the activity of sharing enthusiasm gives rise to rich and complex dimensions. The same sentiment can be applied to "influence". The manifold ways people exercise influence on each other, in combination with the conditions that render influence at its most effective, have for dozens of years, provided a rich vein of study-material for psychologists and economists alike. It is also feasible to develop a relatively uncomplicated metric to be used during research.

In order to determine whether an enthusiastic person is also influential we make use of Influence Metrics (IFMs). IFMs can be either general in scope, or designed with a specific purpose and focused on a particular product or service.

Influence in general

There exist several ways to determine whether someone is an influencer. In some cases, influence comes dressed in the formal garb of someone's executive position in an organization, or perhaps their social status. We grant our sporting greats the power to impress us, which therein makes them influential. A simple measurement of influence in these examples would be the number of people reporting to our executive, or the number of fans cheering on our sports hero.

Another way to measure influence is by posing indirect questions. There already exists a large toolbox of questions available with which to measure influence. Many of these are derived from assessments performed to determine whether people might be suited for leadership positions. After all, people in leadership positions must have influence to do their job properly. The reason for asking indirect questions is because doing otherwise carries the risk of soliciting socially desirable answers from respondents. It is easy to picture someone who does not carry a lot of clout, but wants to come across as one who does, saying that they are influential. Conversely, the modest man of influence will tut-tut and say it's all not that much... Both answers can be considered socially desirable but neither can be considered truthful. Indirect questions are an attempt to filter out the influence of saying things that are socially desirable.

Examples of questions used to measure influence

1. In groups I am often the main contact
2. I manage to be convincing to other people
3. My experience is that people are interested in my opinions

Influence in specific situations

You can ask direct questions about influence in order to learn more about the role of influencing for specific products or services. There is nothing wrong with asking the fan of a given radio programme whether anybody in his environment started to listen as well because of him. The Trollbeads superpromoter of their bracelets from Chapter 3 was not bothered a bit about telling us that she had persuaded at least six girlfriends to start wearing the jewelry as well. The superpromoter in these examples is citing facts and can leave social desirability aside.

We recently found a good example of the way in which superpromoters can wield influence in specific situations. It involved an interview with a Paradontax (toothpaste brand with a non-minty flavor – an acquired taste) customer. She told us that she would never spend the night anywhere without knowing that she had her favorite toothpaste at hand. Being certain of fresh breath was obviously of great significance to her. It was interesting to note that she didn't much like the taste of Paradontax, unlike so many others who like it for its non-mintyness. In fact, the horrid flavor was to her an essential part of the experience; it confirmed to her that her mouth had been scrubbed clean. During the interview she told us that she had convinced a number of friends to at least try the toothpaste, some of whom now also turned into avid fans. For her, an important moment of influential power occurred the morning after. If her new lover had no toothpaste (not something that would ever happen to her!), she seizes her opportunity. Some of her ex-boyfriends have been condemned to a lifelong Paradontax-habit. Some superpromoters have no mercy...!

IDENTIFYING THE ANTIPROMOTER

If you are trying to develop a good overall picture of the influencers among a population of customers, you have to track down the antipromoters as well.

Let us revisit the definition of antipromoter for a moment:

The antipromoter is decidedly negative, shares this negativity with others and thereby influences his social environment.

Accordingly, antipromoters will demonstrate the following three characteristics:

1. An antipromoter is pronouncedly negative
2. An antipromoter shares this negative view around
3. An antipromoter has influence

As is the case with superpromoters, there are three criteria that must be met to make someone into an antipromoter. That means that we will need three metrics to determine

149

whether someone can be classified as an antipromoter:

1. **AM** (Animosity Metric)
2. **SSM** (Social Sharing Metric)
3. **IFM** (Influence Metric)

The main difference with the metrics for superpromoters lies in the Animosity Metric (AM), which measure the degree to which someone is inclined to discourage use of a product. It is possible, however, to also ask the same type of satisfaction and loyalty questions that are used in situations where active discouragement is not the issue (monopolies for example). The "very dissatisfied" category meets the AM criterion.

Which AM, SSM and IFM will be most suitable for surveying the antipromoter will be entirely dependent on the situation.

IN CONCLUSION... AND PEEKING FORWARD

In this chapter we have been looking at the various metrics that are needed to identify superpromoters and antipromoters. If a survey method uses the NPS®, then the proportion of promoters can be taken as an EM (enthusiasm metric). If you incorporate measurements of enthusiasm (SSM) and influence (IFM) it is possible to identify your superpromoters. To identify your antipromoters we will need to use the animosity metric (AM), combined with an SSM and IFM.

The next chapter will be taking a look at a model that you can use for working with your superpromoters. Once the metrics have been established, we'll start to work on the Odilia method, and then go and meet your own superpromoters....

5

GETTING TO WORK WITH ODILIA

INTRODUCTION

Now let's get to work: we've got to know our superpromoters fairly well, and have seen what their role is in the
evolution of our thinking about customer orientation. The
thing that makes it all really interesting, after all, is getting
down to work with your own superpromoters. That's when
it becomes clear how much energy and inspiration a superpromoter has to offer. It can be a significant competitive
advantage to businesses if they understand their superpromoters well and know how to find creative ways of working
with them. This chapter will introduce you to a practical
model, both for getting to know your superpromoters, and
assisting them to exercise influence on their social environment. We call this model **Odilia**.

Odilia is an acronym for:

1. Orientation: Desk research & Internet research
2. **Definition:** Determining which superpromoters are
   important
3. Invitation: Get together with your superpromoters for you to
   talk with them
4. Listening: Letting the superpromoter express their thoughts
   and social experiences

5. Interpretation: Analyzing and interpreting the superpromoter's enthusiasm and the reactions of the social environment
6. Assisting: Helping the superpromoter influence others

THE PRELIMINARY PHASE (ORIENTATION, DEFINITION AND INVITATION)

Orientation

Once you've become interested in superpromoters and have decided to identify and get to know the ones that are relevant to you, the first thing to do is to plough through all of the information that is readily available. Two sources of information are immediately available to you: the Web and customer information already held within the company. Searching the internet is something everyone can get started with at once, without the need to involve others... so it seems obvious to start with this avenue here, too.

Internet research
Both your superpromoters and antipromoters can be tracked down on the web if you know where to look. Via blogs, Twitter, social network sites and a large variety of message boards, people are talking about products and brands all the time. Every day more than 100,000 weblogs are started where people go to share information... what don't they share today? They write not only about their hobbies, work, but also about the things they buy. There is an immense amount of information out there on companies and their brands. As a percentage of the overall population, people who leave messages on websites may not be that large, but

the absolute number of messages is huge and the growth rate is quite staggering. It is an important fact to note that superpromoters leave messages significantly more often than the average web surfer. When they are talking about your product or brand online, it is very good idea to listen to what they are saying. On social network sites like Facebook it is easy to locate brand fans (see Table 5.1). There are now sophisticated search engines that trawl through blogs, message boards and social network sites and flag

Rank	Website	Facebook Fans
1	Facebook	16,921,262
2	Starbucks Coffee	12,778,572
3	YouTube	11,654,221
4	Coca-Cola	10,784,939
5	Red Bull	7,798,746
6	Victoria's Secret	6,378,739
7	Disney	5,828,843
8	ZARA	4,375,746
9	NBA	4,183,189
10	Converse	3,956,735
11	MTV	3,812,486
12	Pixar	3,356,174
13	H&M	3,242,698
14	Monster Energy	3,021,085
15	Chick-fil-A	2,887,672
16	McDonald's	2,739,456
17	Buffalo Wild Wings	2,354,158
18	Taco Bell	2,339,813
19	Kohl's	2,148,518
20	PUMA	2,114,888

Source: http://fanpagelist.com/category/corporate_brands/
Updated: 19th August 2010

Table 5.1 Top corporate brands on Facebook, August 2010

when a certain brand name is mentioned. Of course the essential part is to interpret the messages correctly; sending data up the hierarchy where it can be turned into meaningful information, or even better: intelligence! There is a difference between leaving messages because you're bored or because you're enthusiastic. By the same logic you have to separate your antipromoters from those who are simply making a complaint.

Desk research
Most companies will have accumulated a fair amount of information on their customers over the course of many years. It comes in the shape of customer-satisfaction surveys, feedback via email or – we should not forget this – snail mail, recorded telephone calls received at call centers and so on and so forth. Some companies even get Christmas cards from their customers, or thank-you notes. It can be quite a surprise to discover just how much information is already there, once you start looking. There was one energy company, for example, that discovered it had received a lot of written thank-yous from customers telling them what a nice day they'd had at the zoo. The company had run a campaign a little earlier where their customers could get free tickets for the zoo. Now, it seems highly likely that people who had bothered to send a note would also have been speaking about it within their social environment circle...with some enthusiasm. This is the kind of information that can help you form a general impression of your superpromoters.

Another method is to conduct subject-specific analyses on previously conducted customer surveys, reviewing the data to identify, for example, that group of customers best described as 'enthusiastic'. By concentrating your attention on this specific group, a profile gradually swims into view and the identity of a superpromoter will be revealed. Similarly, studying the angry reactions from disappointed customers helps to define the personality of the antipromoter. In addition to internal survey results, there is another large body of evidence to investigate in other company-based resources: industry data and in-house research material, and the CRM database represent a treasure trove of interesting information. Furthermore, the research phase allows you to identify which facets of customer interaction are important from the customer's point of view; specifically which are the ones where customers are more likely to become enthusiastic, or disappointed?

The orientation phase involving desk research need not be either costly or time-consuming, yet it can be a most valuable exercise. Among other things, the information collected can be extremely helpful in convincing the rest of your organization of the actual existence of your superpromoters. For example, one of the large Dutch banks was initially not terribly convinced that they had any superpromoters. When it was discovered that at the Hyves site literally hundreds of thousands of people had flagged them as their favorite brand, their blindness was cured... Here was a large group of customers proclaiming their enthusiasm, but nobody was listening!

Definition

Having accumulated all available information from the internet and from all the hidden corners of your company, it is time for the next step. This is the time to start creating a clear picture of your business's superpromoters and anti-promoters: Where should you focus your attention? The object of the exercise is to identify which groups are most relevant to you. This will certainly include your customers but your employees, managers, and other executives within the organization are equally good candidates. Reaching beyond, trade unions, journalists and other types of opinion leaders may all exert considerable influence and should be considered.

Picking your battleground carefully, you also must decide which kind of antipromoter is your primary target. If your objective is to recapture disappointed customers for your business, this will require a different strategy from when you are training your sights on the competition's superpromoters. Two important strategic objectives have to be to prevent new antipromoters from joining the ranks in the future, and to identify and search out those antipromoters that can do the most damage. Regrettably, if the gap caused by negative emotions has grown too wide, you may not be able to contact them anymore. But in this case independent outsiders can still talk to them and at least find out how to implement damage control.

We talked in Chapter 2 about the differences between people defined as natural-born superpromoters and situational superpromoters, concluding that both kinds are relevant and useful. When businesses are trying to develop new markets or products, the natural-born superpromoter will be a powerful partner to have on your side. The situational superpromoter who is enthusiastic about your product or brand can, on the other hand, be useful for helping to grow your current product range and is an ideal coach, motivator and source of inspiration. Obviously, a business may have several different groups of situational superpromoters, as a result of it selling different products and services or owning various different brands. Keeping your situational superpromoters separate yet clearly identified is important. Provided the different groups have been adequately identified and defined, it then becomes feasible to search for your superpromoters in a highly focused manner.

Invitation

Well, what are we waiting for? Now that we have figured out who our superpromoters are, it's time to invite them to participate. If, during the desk research phase it has become fairly clear to you where your superpromoters are located, the thing to do is to contact them directly right there and then. For example, if you have customer surveys in progress, or have a regular research program, it is possible to add questions to your existing surveys to identify and engage superpromoters. There are other natural contact points with customers, which may be used to identify and engage superpromoters. A typical example would be a help desk. Remember it can be during these precise moments of contact where superpromoters and antipromoters are spawned. We've all seen those consumer-TV shows full of customers' horror stories with call centers and help desks. Notice how these programmes never let the enthusiastic customers tell their story...

There are many businesses that measure complaints-handling by asking customers a few questions after their contact. Software programmes often prompt the questions. This is the time to pin down the superpromoters and feed back their enthusiastic reactions. Because it is a fairly straightforward exercise to separate superpromoters from regular customers, by asking a few questions, it has become possible during, say, a marketing campaign, to pinpoint your superpromoters and engage them in dialogue. *Logica* and *Oracle* have both developed software programmes to make it easier to identify a superpromoter during a marketing campaign. Having identified the superpromoter they are given special treatment; they get to jump a queue of callers on hold, and the call centre operative is given more time to speak with them. At this point they are invited to participate in a discussion forum or to join a panel with other superpromoters. In order to demonstrate how the software works the managers of a well-known pop star built a business case to try out the system using the following fictitious scenario:

Just imagine for a moment that famous pop-singer XYZ is planning to make a movie. But for now it's an open question how his fans are going to react to the news that their XYZ has developed acting aspirations. To keep a finger on the pulse of his public, they set up a toll-free phone number plus website to coincide with the start of the movie's PR-campaign. Here his fans can leave their feedback on his plans. When his fans call in or visit the website, they are first asked a few questions to identify whether they are a superpromoter. These are the questions:

- Would you recommend XYZ's music to your friends and acquaintances?
- Do you ever talk to your friends about XYZ's music?
- Did any of your friends start to listen (more) to XYZ's music because of you?

If someone answers "yes" to all three questions they are flagged as a superpromoter. XYZ's managers pay close attention to input coming from these identified superpromoters; they could, after all, make or break the success of the campaign for his new movie. If this group isn't happy, the campaign will be revised. This group of superpromoters is directed toward a restricted website where they can contribute their ideas for the revisions required for the campaign. This way the managers don't even have to figure it out for themselves! The website has a forum where they can discuss issues and ideas, and react to questions thrown out at them by the pop star's managers. If, for example, XYZ is doing a talk show, his managers can follow live what's kind of reactions are being given in the forum and even provide additional explanation if one of XYZ's answers on the talk show wasn't understood properly. Our singer could even be told through his earpiece and could give a live reaction if this seemed appropriate. The forum is where superpromoters can put forward their comments and suggestions on how to improve the campaign. If things go well, as they should, two important results occur: first, the campaign is improved and will have greater impact, second, the involvement of superpromoters in the process makes them even more enthusiastic, and they will be telling everybody they know about all about it...very enthusiastically.

LISTENING

Let's take a look at how best to listen to the superpromoter. One way would be through direct personal conversation. Another involves the creation of a panel or community of superpromoters. Finding out the roots of enthusiasm requires careful listening. It also tells you how your super-promoters share their enthusiasm and how they work their influence on others. First we focus on how the conversation flows while we are getting to know our superpromoter better. At this point, we must be aware of the difference between conversations that take place in a professional business setting and conversations with consumers. Talking with consumers is very different from talking with professionals and therefore demands different skills.

Figuring out the enthusiasm of a business-professional superpromoter

In a professional business setting, the interviewer must also be an experienced professional. This would give the customer the sense that he knows what he is talking about, so that as interviewee they can have a pleasant and meaningful experience. Normally speaking, the conversation would get started with the client providing a description of his relationship with the seller/service provider as seen from his perspective. We get to see whether we're dealing with an enthusiastic customer as soon as they start talking about the product, or brand or service. It is of course the interviewer's job to find out how their enthusiasm came about. In one example, the client of a law firm told us that his enthusiasm was based on a positive experience several years before. The client was grateful for the fact that the law firm had burned the midnight oil to solve his problem for him...over Christmas, no less. The law firm had earned lots of kudos with this job and the happy client had referred several new clients to the firm. That piece of information turned out to be news to the lawyers; they knew of his enthusiasm for a job well done, but not that he had repaid them with his referrals. The information uncovered in this one conversation was a great opportunity to give another pat on the back to the team that, back then, had worked through the night, several times. If a client is not a superpromoter but is responsible for a lot of turnover, this kind of conversation can be used to discover why a customer is not enthusiastic (any longer) and what can be done to turn things around (again). The business-professional superpromoter is usually also perfectly capable of participating in strategic discussions, such as how a firm should be positioning itself. In another example, a customer indicated that his service provider had a strong presence among small to medium sized firms, but that he had noticed they were beginning to focus their marketing efforts more and more on the larger, listed companies. This superpromoter thought this was a very bad idea: he thought they would be far better off concentrating their efforts on the smaller and mid-sized customer groups. Better a big fish in a smaller pond than a smaller fish in a bigger pond was his opinion. This happened to be precisely the positioning question the service providers were grappling with! And here was a superpromoter who had a very clear and outspoken set of ideas!

Talking to your superpromoters can be most enriching, not just for the information you glean, but also because talking with them firsthand is inspirational. When the dialogue takes place in a professional setting, it also acts as an aspect of customer relationship management. Experienced interviewers, however, will have the experience and know-how to dig deeper into the complexities of enthusiasm, shared enthusiasm and influence. There is one other reason to be making use of external interviewers, which is that most interviewees can be a bit more reticent when talking to a representative of the business itself. In this case there is a tendency then to soften their criticism and not address their smaller irritations. Their enthusiasm also tends to remain partially under wraps. Even the most assertive superpromoter will be much more explicit toward an independent third party. Most of us are taught from early on not to express our frustrations or enthusiasms directly to the party responsible; both are more readily expressed to a third party.

How does a business-professional superpromoter share his enthusiasm?
Networks operating both inside and outside a business play an important role in sharing enthusiasm. There are formal networks within the company, such as the hierarchical lines of command and the collaborative traditions among several departments. The formal lines outside the company tend to be professional industry associations or other types of networking structures. Separate from the formal circuit, there also exists a large and no less important informal circuit. It is within these channels that advice is shared and recommendations made about suppliers and service providers. Superpromoters exert influence on potential customers within these networks with the power of their enthusiasm. Our job is to understand in depth how these social networks function, and how enthusiasm is shared amongst participants.

It is only in conversation with customers that it becomes clear how complex the sharing of enthusiasm can become. Some service providers have discovered they can be given both a thumbs up and thumbs down by the same customer. All sorts of things carry weight: the competition and what they are doing is relevant, personal relationships with contacts are important, and all of these aspects are constantly in a state of flux. These are all good reasons for keeping in touch with your most important superpromoters, and the best way of keeping abreast of the latest developments. This way you can stay on top of your relationship with them and find out how the rest of their social network thinks about you, and what's happening in the marketplace.

Influence in a business setting

A third characteristic of superpromoters is their level of influence. In an ordinary business environment formal influence is strictly governed by many rules. There is always a chain of command: an employee submits a request for a new computer to his Department Head, who, in turn, submits the appropriate forms (in triplicate) to the Head of Office Supplies & Services, who, in turn, prepares a purchase order for the Head of Purchasing: a typical example of a bureaucracy where influence is well defined. As always, even here reality is somewhat more complex. As we all know, aside from our formal channels, we all work with informal channels . . . probably just as much and sometimes more. It is possible however to uncover valuable information when confining oneself to a survey of formal channels only. During one interview with a large customer of a service provider it soon became clear that the personal relationship between the customer's two employees and the service provider was sufficiently close that switching was just not on the cards. The customer's representative was going to be taking early retirement in a few years, and it seemed like a good possibility that his successor might select a different provider. His suggestion to the provider was to start planning ahead, and develop a broader and deeper relationship with his employees straight away, in anticipation of the winds of change that sooner or later would come sweeping through. This was a superpromoter giving valuable advice! We found a similar example in a survey involving the head of a painting & decorating firm. He told us he was planning to hand over the firm to his son in a few years' time and felt that he ought to give him complete freedom in his selection of external advisors. Yet, at that moment he could still exert quite a lot of influence on the decisions his son would soon be making, something to take into timely consideration.

Furthermore, how people exercise their influence is always an interesting topic of conversation. Is the boss a despot? Or does he give his people enough space to participate in decision-making about the company's service providers? You could look at this another way with the question: which people exercise influence because of their formal role, and which because of their powers of persuasion?

From these types of conversations we can also get a good idea of how valuable a customer might be as a superpromoter. Some might seem of modest value at first glance, but then turn out to be valuable ambassadors. It wouldn't be the first time that a group of customers viewed as "insignificant" by the company have a knock-on effect on sales because of the many recommendations they give. They might have brought in lots of business with their enthusiasm. When we learn about these things from interviews with superpromoters, after swallowing hard, your image of that client changes forever!

The origins of enthusiasm among consumers
It is always fun to be talking to consumers of something they are enthusiastic about. In those situations, it hardly ever takes any prodding to get them fully fired up about "their" product or service. In contrast, finding out where their enthusiasm came from is a little more challenging. Here we have to take account of the emotional, and perhaps even irrational factors at play, some of which the customer isn't fully aware of, if at all.

Nevertheless, from interviews with consumers we do get a glimpse of the psychological relationship people may have with brands, products or services. As we've said, consumers don't always have a focused understanding of what made them choose one product over another. Whatever motivation they can come up with is always *ex post* reasoning.[39] When was the last time you justified an impulse-buy afterward? We all do. During consumer interviews our job has to be to peel the onion of psychological motivations layer by layer, perhaps never really grasping all of the various factors that have been playing a role, or to what extent. Neither the average consumer, nor any of us, really, has the kind of brain that can keep track of these things: advertising, earlier experiences, recommendations we received, rational comparisons, and so on. One thing we can say about superpromoters is that they seem to be a bit more alert to the choices they make than average people. Their enthusiasm makes them more aware, they are more likely to be actively looking for information and the superpromoter will have better insights. Someone who is truly enthusiastic will also be able to talk about a product more readily. This is how we can eventually uncover in conversation what made them enthusiastic in the first place. If during a survey you have a consumer who is not very involved with the product, and hence, the topic, it is much more difficult to extract the teeth of information you need. Superpromoters are an easier read, although it always remains a bit of an art and a science to analyze the source of enthusiasm. But better to have a superpromoter on your couch if you're the one doing the analysis!

Consumers and sharing enthusiasm

Shared enthusiasm is always a complex issue to investigate, and so it is in the world of consumers as well. Amongst consumers, you can also find someone making recommendations, or doing the reverse. It even happens that sometimes they give the same person the thumbs up and thumbs down (though not at the same time, hopefully)! If you want to go abroad on vacation and be sure of high quality child minding, many people will recommend Club Med to you. But if you don't want to sleep in one room with your kids, or speak French at the table with your fellow diners, you shouldn't go. Conclusion: you have to have an idea of what the consumer's social needs are if you want to learn about the ways that enthusiasm can be shared. Is it spontaneous, or is it discussed only within the context of a given occasion? Mortgages, for example, are likely to be a source of conversation while you are buying a house, but afterward, interest in the topic fades. Another thing to look at is whether the consumer is mainly talking about subjects in a negative – complaining – manner or gets involved more in optimistic conversations? All people need to have social contact; it is one of life's basic necessities. And social intercourse is all about talking with each other about this, that, and the other...in social settings we're always looking for topics to talk about. This means that people tend to be quite open to experiences they can get enthusiastic about, because they represent valuable ammunition for topics of conversation. Accordingly, having a debate in which people share their enthusiasm is bound to offer you some valuable insights. Some consumers limit themselves to a fairly small circle of friends, whereas with others it spans across dozens of friends, family members as well as people at work. Where this sharing of enthusiasm takes place is also of interest. We spoke before about recommendations that were being given at the hairdressers'. Location, location, location, it can mean a lot. Sometimes, the place where enthusiasm is shared can be a more formal or organized setting, such as happens in book clubs or reading circles, for example.

Influence among consumers

Not every consumer carries the same amount of influence in his environment. Every group has its key personalities, the people you talk to when you want to find out about something, or get advice. They are the people who are in the know about buying a new car, where the best bakery is, or what to put where on your tax returns. They have a certain status that is recognized by others; they are both convincing and believable. Our interest is in finding out how influence is being exercised. Are superpromoters people who go forth and tell others what to do, or do those others more or less come to them for advice unasked? Usually superpromoters can give you concrete examples of influencing others and what the result was. The video clip on superpromoters[40] we cited as an example earlier shows the Trollbeads superpromoter giving very concrete examples of how she influenced her neighbor and girlfriends. When her friends tell her they

167

think it's too expensive, she tells them to buy the basic kit first and slowly grow their collection afterwards, exactly the same as any good sales person would be doing. Our superpromoter in this instance can tell us exactly how she goes about influencing her social network.

The antipromoter speaks

It is obviously also relevant to know what antipromoters have to say. This is even more to the point if your antipromoter happens to be a former superpromoter: you must find out why they changed their opinions. If they have become superpromoters for the competition, your job is to find out why that competitor is performing better, at least in the eyes of your antipromoter. Summing up, everything we've been saying about superpromoters also applies to antipromoters. So...we need to find out what their negative opinion is based upon, how they are sharing it with their social surroundings, and also how they exercise influence on the world around them. Interviews with antipromoters are also better conducted by independent interviewers. What causes the antipromoters to be what they are finds its most unfettered expression when they are given the opportunity to speak, and social conventions such as politeness will not form any obstacle with a competent interviewer.

Listening to superpromoters in panels and communities

There are several different ways of getting to know the superpromoter better. Talking with them is the most obvious, but monitoring them during regular surveys and other contact moments may all be suitable occasions. There are also ways of developing a closer connection with superpromoters; for example, by bringing them together in consumer panels or communities. Superpromoters are friendly and always have time to give their advice. Additionally, it is good to remember that, because they are focused on their social surroundings they have a keen sense of what's going on out there in the market. So it can be a very nice thing to have your superpromoter available "on tap" to be able to ask them what they think at any time. This is where a panel of superpromoters comes in...it's a bit like having a direct help line to a call centre full of very smart friends. Superpromoters – this should not come as a surprise – have an above average willingness to sit on these panels, as they are enthusiastic, and like to be involved. The basic difference between a panel and a community is that with panels, interaction among panel members is avoided as much as possible. The idea is to obtain "pure" information from each, untainted by them influencing each other. If there is too much interaction among panel members, it may cause them to become "atypical" representatives of exactly what you are studying. In a community, on the other hand, the whole idea is to have lots of contact between members. They can ask questions of each other and respond at any time. One of the advantages of a community is that it gives you an immediate insight into the superpromoter's social interaction, whether it be chatting, email or a discussion forum. In terms of structure, communities can be compared to social networking sites such as Hyves or My Space. We normally bring together superpromoters of a specific brand or product into a community. Not only is it a platform where superpromoters can communicate with each other, but it also represents their opportunity to communicate with the company they love. A community can be managed and exploited online, but your superpromoters could also be invited to a physical meeting or to attend a special event.

The superpromoter recorded on video
It is simple, effective and therefore astonishingly valuable to have superpromoters tell you on videotape why they are such enthusiasts. There's nothing like visual aids to show you how infectious enthusiasm can be. Just hand them a microphone and let them talk for a while. In fact, when you are recording an interview, it will feel more spontaneous if you let the superpromoters tell their own story as much as possible. Merely answering questions is not that exciting. There are several examples of these types of videoclips to be found at www.superpromoters.com. While viewing these clips, the first thing you'll notice is how infectious their enthusiasm is...even if the product they're talking about doesn't mean anything to you.

The people working for the same company as the super-promoting star of a videoclip are always particularly excited. When they are shown a clip of their own superpromoters everyone is sitting on the edge of their seats. Watching these videos can be a very exciting experience and a strong motivator to others in the company. They provide a clear visual illustration of why customers get enthusiastic about their product. Knowing what makes your customers happy means knowing what to aim for. These instructional video-clips are easily distributed and can be used over and over. In our experience with companies large and small, every-body, from top to bottom of the organization, wants to see these clips. Does this sound like a highly positive and effective way of introducing viral buzz about the superpromoter into the works of an organization?

It isn't just the fact that visual media are such a powerful force that makes videoclips so inspirational. It doesn't hurt, of course, but what is surely equally inspirational is the fact that the superpromoter very clearly means you well. Hearing from somebody about the things you happen to be doing well can be very inspirational, it gives you the energy and confirmation you need to carry on. And if it turns out that you are given a couple of pointers on what to do better, you can take those in your stride as well. This can be such a different experience from having to listen to a customer complaining about the trivial (at least in the eyes of the listener) shortcomings of a product, having worked like dogs to try to make him happy. This is the type of customer experience most workers are confronted with, and probably helps to explain why people working in larger companies in particular often have the feeling that their customers feel much worse about them than is actually the case. Their overdose of negative feedback can give them a distorted picture of reality.

Survey questionnaires

It is certainly not the case that our superpromoter can only be tracked down with the most modern research tools. The traditional questionnaire used in surveys is still a suitable tool for getting to know them a little better. This way of collecting information about them has a secondary benefit that most superpromoters are usually very much inclined to cooperate with your survey. Today, as response rates for all types of surveys are declining, this is a valuable asset to have. But it is important not to fall into the trap of setting up the survey as if it is standard piece of customer-satisfaction research. For this investigation to be useful, it must focus on the sources of enthusiasm, and how enthusiasm is transferred by sharing it around. This is not only the most important element to consider, but this approach also makes the survey more reliable. Superpromoters are better capable than the average consumer of explaining their own behavior, not to mention the fact that they are good at observing their environment. In fact, because they are such social creatures, they are echoing just what they do in their entire life! People like this have accumulated a great deal of social data in their subconscious, which allows them to make pretty accurate estimates of their environment's likely response to new products and services. This is a characteristic that serves us well when we are investigating superpromoters.

INTERPRETATION

We've done our homework, we've listened carefully to the superpromoters, the time has now come to lay all of our information out on the table and start interpreting what we have learned: what we've seen online, the internal data, what employees have said, and what superpromoters and antipromoters themselves have told us. Incorporating all of this will get us closer to the truth of what lies behind the enthusiasm of superpromoters…and the frustrations of antipromoters. At this stage we are beginning to understand how enthusiasm and disappointment is shared within social surroundings and we have a handle on the techniques used for wielding influence. Finally, in order to find out why enthusiasm can sometimes remain extremely localized and at other times set the whole world on fire, we need to understand the structure of the social networks of superpromoters.

Understanding the origin and transfer of enthusiasm

The source of enthusiasm must be understood if we are going to assist our superpromoters in remaining enthusiastic and continuing to wield influence over others. The first thing we need to be aware of is that among other things, the sources of enthusiasm have psychological, sociological, cultural and economic determinants. Whether someone is extroverted plays a role of course, but also what type of friends they have, the culture they live in, and their relative wealth (or poverty). In the poorer regions people's enthusiasm may be fired by life's bare necessities much more than in our affluent western society.

We have identified a number of possible stimulants for enthusiasm in Chapter 2.

• New and Original products/services
• Events that cause a "Positive Surprise"
• A context of "Authenticity"
• Products/services that Promote Social Contacts
• Products/services that are Practical, Problem-solving, or perhaps just plain Better
• Relationships that are Open, Transparent and Honest
• Products/services that are Beautiful and Compelling
• And then there's value for money!

During this phase we have to identify these types of stimulants when we're investigating the sources of enthusiasm. The superpromoters have had their say and explained to us what made them enthusiastic; our turn now to interpret this information. For example, what were the superpromoter's expectations? If we can meet, or even better, exceed their expectations, they will remain enthusiastic. Is your company able to meet your superpromoters' minimum expectations, and do better with some regularity, at least?

At this moment in time Apple has probably more superpromoters than any other company in the world. Pretty much everybody knows someone in his or her social circle who praises Apple to high heaven. Yet it would seem as if our ubiquitously praised fruit might be developing some bruises because of the company's excessively protectionist stance. IPhone's options are only accessible through certain suppliers; the Ipod and Iphone software is protected, meaning that its users cannot tailor make anything to their specifications. The original Apple superpromoters – on the whole belonging to the more revolutionary group of users of computer hardware – could be turning against Apple as a result of the company's attitude. This development could give rise to a generation of antipromoters that could be adopted by an Apple competitor with a more open-minded approach. If Apple pays close attention to its superpromoters and takes action on time, its heydays have long to live. If not, even super companies like Apple could lose the support of their superpromoters.

During this stage we must also be able to form a picture of how enthusiasm gets shared. Which sharing mechanisms play a role? Is word-of-mouth behavior spontaneous, or merely passive? To what extent does (subconscious) herd behavior play a role? The many ways in which enthusiasm gets passed around have been described at various stages of our story.

Influence and the role of the social environment
Superpromoters can only wield influence if others take them seriously. In Chapter 2 we discussed the many ways in which influence can be exerted. From listening carefully to superpromoters we can learn which of these methods

they use. Not that they can control the influence they are able to wield entirely by themselves; the superpromoter can only function well if their social environment is responsive to their influence.

This is the reason why at this stage we study enthusiasm's infectiousness from the perspective of the recipient. Because the infrastructure of a superpromoter's social network can equally serve to weaken or strengthen his influence, it is important for the company to investigate whether their superpromoter's network is receptive to his influence. If it is receptive, that might make the difference between having a company with a stable group of loyal customers or one with exponential growth.

Is the world ready for it?

On the one side we have superpromoters who are trying to influence their world with their enthusiasm. Yet, in order for that influence to have any impact their social networks must be willing to be influenced. Products don't get hyped without masses of people buying into that hype. In his 2003 book, *Six Degrees: The Science of a Connected Age*, Duncan Watts[41] compares this social interaction to the spread of a wildfire. You can light a match, but not much will happen if the forest is damp...when really dry however, you get to see why they call it "spreading like wildfire". The same applies to a superpromoter, who can only ignite others with their enthusiasm when their social environment is receptive. The bad news is that the same applies to antipromoters, who carry a far larger matchstick during times when their social circle is fearful and desperate for information and advice. These words being written during the "Credit Crunch", this period represents a much easier time for antipromoters to discourage people from making investments – in real estate, or buy-to-let, say – than before the financial crisis.

In *Six Degrees*, Duncan Watts tells us what criteria a social network must meet if it is to be an instrument of mass-distribution of something, be it product, hype, rage, ideas and so on. The book's title is a reference to the Small World experiments conducted by Stanley Milgram in 1967, which suggested that everyone in the world (or, at least in the US) was separated from everyone else by only six steps. Milgram only used the term 'Small World' experiment, but his theory had a superpromoter called John Guare, who made it famous in his play, *Six Degrees of Separation*. In Milgram's experiment a couple of hundred random Americans from the Mid West were sent an information package with a letter to be forwarded to a specific stockbroker in Boston, Mass. If the random participants happened to know the stockbroker, they could forward the letter directly; in the more likely case they did not, they were asked to forward it to that person they knew who would most likely bring the letter closer to the stockbroker in Boston. Milgram's purpose was to find out how many steps this would take, and it turned out to be six (approximately). Over the years there have been many potshots taken at the experiments. Some were deserved, but the basic premise has never been invalidated. Most everybody on this globe is indeed removed from every other person by only half a dozen or so steps, the more so in our age of interconnectivity thanks to the web and globalization. And this development can be thanked for the exponential growth rates described earlier in *The Superpromoter*.

Let's imagine that we all have one hundred friends and acquaintances; probably a conservative estimate if you add in all of your former classmates, neighbors, colleagues, web-friends and the like. It would mean that everyone would have approximately 10,000 friends of friends and a million friends of friends of friends. This would, strictly speaking, not quite add up, since these cannot be "net" numbers: in real life there will be a great deal of overlap among networks of friends; that number of one million friends of friend of friends is not composed of different people entirely. But the overlap does not change the fact that (except for cave dwelling hermits) you will capture the world's population in six jumps on average.

So, people's social connectivity really knows no bounds and this is even truer in the age of Hyves, Facebook, LinkedIn and My Space. LinkedIn can give you a fine picture of how complete strangers will often be only three or four steps removed from you. Back to the Milgram experiment, one interesting finding in the experiment was that most of the letters making it to the stockbroker in the end came funneled through only a handful of the same people. It seems that every social network has certain key contact points that play a far more important role in disseminating information than the average person. They are the influencers, who, when enthusiastic about something, are transformed into superpromoters.

When does enthusiasm break out and infect the masses? According to Duncan Watts it depends pretty much on network criteria: its structure and scope. It has to do with the number of connections, the different dimensions by which people become connected and with people's threshold, in other words, their susceptibility for a given idea. If the threshold is low, susceptibility is high.

The threshold of susceptibility

During the days when the PC did not yet pack a lot of protection by way of virus scanners and firewalls, the threshold for invasion by a computer virus was low and susceptibility to infection high. There existed viruses in those days that might have caused a worldwide PC pandemic had they struck. Nowadays that threshold has been elevated considerably with all the protection available. Similarly, you might say for consumers that their threshold for advertising has been built up. Twenty years or so ago people used to take advertising messages more seriously than today. Today's global citizen has become sufficiently media-smart that an advertising campaign does not carry the same type of impact anymore. Smart marketing and advertising people have been pondering how to overcome this problem, with occasional moments of significant success. We know that the chances that a new product, idea or virus spreads like wildfire around the world depends on whether the social network that is to carry the message is susceptible. There have been moments – aided by modern media – that information has spread around the globe much faster even than wildfire. How long did it take before you knew that an airplane had crashed into the World Trade Center? Not much of a chance that it took more than 24 hours for the news to reach you, wherever you were. For many, many people, the experience was viewed live. Yes, modern media were able to distribute the information much faster than, say, news of the assassination of Abraham Lincoln on April 14, 1865. Nonetheless, most people first heard the 9/11 news from another person and not first from radio or TV. This was news of a magnitude that everyone needed to talk about it, the susceptibility of this message was as high as it can get.

Too many or to few friends

Social networks have a very high degree of mathematical complexity. The theory of networks represents a specialization within the field of mathematics only accessible to those with the best brains. An important predictor of the chances that enthusiasm will spread is the number of connections that people have to each other. Without a critical mass of connections an idea will not get very far. An example of this occurs whenever a group of people is isolated from others. Isolated may mean living on a desert island without means of communication beyond the message in a bottle, but clearly, people may also be socially isolated. This is the thing that is often the case with older people whose mobility is reduced while their social network has been dying out, literally. Some groups of people choose to live in isolation; terrorists and religious sects come to mind. Lacking any form of connection to other people, they will not be contributing to the spread of enthusiasm of epidemic proportions. Conversely, too many connections can also snuff out any enthusiasm for an idea before it takes hold. Where there are many connections they tend to be more superficial, which makes it more difficult to wield influence over others because the connection is not strong enough. A nice example of this is the internet, as a people network. Endless numbers of people get in touch with each other online, sending email, spam and so forth. But, if a total stranger sends you even the most enthusiastic message, the chances of it infecting you are pretty slim. Among three close musketeers, however, chances of listening and becoming inspired are 100% (well...almost!). Conclusion: the structure of the network and the total number of connections amongst its contributors are the

key influences of how susceptible we are to a superpromoter's enthusiasm.

The importance of cross connections

The existence of cross connections between social networks
is the other element that is of significant importance to
the ability of enthusiasm to spread like wildfire. Most of us
inhabit several social networks at the same time; carrying
enthusiasm from one to the other contributes to the rapid
spread among different networks. Who hasn't told a joke
heard at work in another network, at home, in the pub, or
to friends at the gym? We know already that those people
who are natural-born superpromoters inhabit several social
circles at the same time, and that they are people who are
listened to. Who better than them to spread a good joke
around? But if we are really to get a joke-epidemic under
way, their friends must also be passing it on to their friends,
and on, and on. At first, the gym can be a suitable breed-
ing ground for it, but very soon everybody there knows the
joke already... "Groan, heard that one before!" We'll need
the people who can tell a joke in different networks for the
virus to spread.

The game of strong and weak social ties

The influence a superpromoter wields is not limited to a
small close-knit social circle of friends. In fact, the influence of a superpromoter on people in the periphery of his
social circle is even greater than on his close friends. The
reason for this is that weak social connections can reach
farther than strong ties. In his 1973 article, "The Strength
of Weak Ties", Mark Granovetter[42] describes how social
ties that are farther removed from a person – a friend of a

friend of a friend – have far greater impact on the way individuals influence each other than close ties. The reasons are twofold: among close friends the overlap of information sources and connections is too great, while the ability to spread influence is much smaller. Friends share the same friends, acquaintances and information, which make it harder to be the bearer of something entirely new. If you are looking for a new job, for example, the chances that someone from outside your close circle will be able to help you is far greater than from within. To a large extent, friends of your direct friends are still the same kind of people. So, asking about a new job will not get you very far because the overlap is too great. Those you barely know, or have only heard of are much more likely to be able to offer good leads.

The spread of information is always going to be fastest where there is fertile ground; among acquaintances, the chances are you don't all hold the same information. Among friends you are sharing mostly the same information. When enthusiasm is being sent to the borders of a social network, it will fly with wings and carry the message to foreign lands...

Until social ties become too weak, because then the risk exists it will spread no more. The influence of a superpromoter wanes as the distance from his core increases. Where he is not known, his message cannot have the same effect. That means that it is important to strike a balance between strong and weak ties. Where enthusiasm can catch on among a small social circle of close friends, outside of that circle its spread will be arrested and not travel far. The reason it catches on so easily within the circle is because people take each other seriously. And that effect gets lost

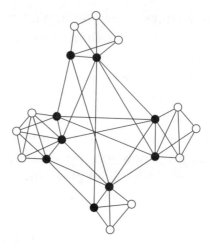

Figure 5.1   Small World Network

when you try to do the same thing with people you barely know. However, when it does jump across to be among people who are less closely connected, it will then spread very rapidly and reach very far. The same dynamics, essentially, as with a real virus. The ideal network takes the form of a Small World Network (see Figure 5.1).

In the perfect world of a Small World Network ties within groups are strong enough, and every group has several connections to other groups. This is the most efficient network structure for spreading something around, because within groups everyone gets infected almost at once, while the connectors among groups cause the infection to jump from group to group. Any one connection will be less important when everyone is connected to everyone else. This is more difficult and therefore inefficient to try to manage. The Small World Network where superpromoters are the connectors among groups are the ideal structure to ensure that enthusiasm can spread around fast and wide.

No enthusiasm without susceptibility

However much a superpromoter is raving with enthusiasm, if it does not find fertile ground in his social environment, the strength of their enthusiasm will diminish. And let's face it; getting others to come onside is what it's all about for superpromoters. If they don't succeed in passing on their enthusiasm for a particular subject, they'll focus their attentions on another subject. Perhaps the world isn't ready for this product yet, or perhaps there's some resistance against it within his social circle. Not that it happens very often that a superpromoter misjudges his environment's willingness to share their enthusiasms. Endowed by nature with a highly developed social intelligence, the superpromoter's decision whether or not to become enthusiastic in the first place is largely determined by his assessment if others will share it. That is a marked difference from other consumers, who only want to try out new technology, for example, because of their personal interest and curiosity. They could be passionate users of new technology, without trying to share it with their friends who are not yet ready for it. The superpromoter on the other hand, tends to become enthusiastic about products they expect to be of interest to their social network. They want to be ahead of their peers, but not by too much. Our conclusion can therefore be that the susceptibility of a superpromoter's social network is a pre-condition to how well it will promote the spread of any given idea. But, in those situations where there are enough superpromoters, and where their social network is susceptible to being influenced by them, then nothing will stop an enthusiasm epidemic from taking off like...uh, wildfire.

In summary:

SUPERPROMOTER + SUSCEPTIBLE SOCIAL NETWORK
= EPIDEMIC OF ENTHUSIASM

ASSISTING THE SUPERPROMOTER

In this section we shall be looking at ways we can offer the superpromoter assistance. We are using the terms *helping*, *assisting* and *supporting* deliberately. The reason is that many companies think that they must buy a superpromoters' support. A good "bad" example of this happens when popular Blogs and Twitterers are offered money for posting supportive blogs or Tweets. Going down that road is dangerous. There lurks the risk that the bribed superpromoter loses their credibility and that their audience will become seriously disappointed by the brand engaging in this type of practice. This is almost certainly the case if the bribery was done sneakily. By far the best way to make sure that a superpromoter will infect as many people as possible is by feeding their enthusiasm, by helping them spread their enthusiasm and by assisting them to influence others. Let's first take a closer look at how we can feed their enthusiasm.

Feeding enthusiasm

The best way of keeping a superpromoter's enthusiasm alive and making it grow is by paying attention to what they are saying and actually doing something with their ideas. Some of the ideas they bring to you can be put to use immediately. For example, if something in your users' manual is confusing or unclear, chances are a superpromoter can tell you about it, and put you on track to fix the problem. Incidentally, superpromoters will not only tell you what they found confusing themselves; they are just as likely to tell you what their mother couldn't understand in the manual. These things can be of indirect importance to a superpromoter. Perhaps he was the one who bought his mom his favorite DVD player and now she doesn't know how to get it working properly. The superpromoter will come to her rescue, but the disappointment is there, and should be remedied if at all possible. If the company takes his suggestions to heart, it will boost the superpromoter's enthusiasm for the brand. In other words, if the company decides to act on a suggestion for improvement made by the superpromoter, it must not forget to communicate this fact. This way the superpromoter will know they are being taken seriously. Feedback is important – in both directions! Explaining why a suggestion is not being taken up is just as important: if they are given a proper explanation why not, the superpromoter might be able to live with it; at least they know they were listened to. It is very important for the superpromoter to be taken seriously, and appreciated...it is the key to their heart.

By that same token, we have to avoid the pitfall of only paying attention to things that might need improving. The nice thing, after all, is that superpromoters can also tell you what you are doing right: do not underestimate the importance of knowing what you are doing well! This is where you should be investing time and energy, and is how you can become a market leader: by using the enthusiasm of the superpromoter! And it's something the superpromoter is willing to cooperate with. They want their enthusiasm to be heard, and their input gives them confidence that the company will be continuing to do that which got him enthusiastic in the first place. The input you get from superpromoters should therefore be shared with as many people as possible in the company, not only does it motivate people, but it also helps them focus on what is positive. Obvious as this may seem, experience tells us that many businesses are not focused enough on the things they are doing right. This is probably the reason why so many companies have started to look the same. They are watching each other carefully and making improvements where they scored lower than their competitors. But it takes more than this to get your superpromoters excited. To distinguish yourself from the herd you must be clearly better, more authentic, and if necessary, also cheaper than your competitors.

One good strategy for keeping your superpromoters happy is to make sure that you exceed their expectations regularly. You'll be able to pick up ideas on how to do this directly from your superpromoters. Often they will be enthusiastic about some aspect of the service or certain features of the product that are not obvious blips on the company's radar screen. Maybe it is something the competition has overlooked, or a particular case where your workers have been really helpful. Happy employees, friendly employees, they are the people capable of random acts of kindness and spontaneous acts that make superpromoters happy. How and where we can exceed our customers' expectations is a good thing to know; as a strategy it is a recipe for success.

Supporting the spread of enthusiasm

Spontaneous word-of-mouth behavior is not something you can manage as a company. At least not directly. When superpromoters make recommendations because they are being paid to do so, it isn't spontaneous anymore. Not only should customers not be made to feel that they are being taken for a ride, but also if superpromoters were to start feeling that the business they are enthusiastic about is only out to get their money, they could turn venomous. All that a company should do is remove any obstacles to the super-promoter's desire to make recommendations. It is always possible that there are obstacles to people recommending you, even if they wanted to. Lack of pertinent information is such an obstacle. So is not knowing what you as a company stand for on a range of issues, or not feeling comfortable with some aspect of the service. The solution of course is information. Make sure that your superpromoters have all the information they'll need, make it easy for them to talk to you. The other ways include focusing specific advertising messages on your superpromoters, organizing special events for them and providing them with samples that could engender their spontaneous word-of-mouth enthusiasm.

A small digression on terminology
Throughout *The Superpromoter* we've been using the term *word of mouth*, sometimes referring to it as *recommending behavior* or something similar. Marketing literature uses a number of terms to describe this aspect of their discipline, usually it's *managed*, or *organized word-of-mouth*, but every marketer by now has heard of *viral* or *buzz* in addition to

word of mouth. We've also seen *brand advocacy*, advergames, *blog marketing*, *influencer panels*, *consumer empowerment*, and the collective, *connected marketing* seeping into the jargon. As long as we understand what we are doing and why, the terminology can take care of itself. The best thing, as always, is to listen to the superpromoters themselves. What do they have to say? They can let you know how they wish to be supported.

Here are a few possibilities on how to support a superpromoter's word of mouth.

1. Managed word-of-mouth: Managing word of mouth means that there is a company directing this form of behavior. Customers feel that they are being helped if they are given information about what other customers are doing (Surely you'll recognize: "Frequently bought together" or "Customers who bought this item also bought"). Much used are testimonials, a perfect example of managed recommendations. Most websites and printed material nowadays make prolific use of this strategy. The testimonial invariably has a satisfied – even enthusiastic – customer saying how happy they are with...If the testimonial comes across as honest and (nearly) spontaneous) it can be a very powerful tool with which to help new customers feel comfortable with product, brand or service.

The word-of-mouth information that is being managed in automated form by websites such as Amazon (they use what you just read in the preceding paragraph) manages to sort through yours and countless other customers' shopping behavior, and tells you live what other customers are doing while you're driving your virtual shopping cart. Amazon was an early adopter of this strategy and gave it an added dimension by capitalizing on people's desire to write (book) reviews on whatever they like. The fact that not all reviews are positive, or that the star-ratings tell you at a glance how something gets ranked, lends credibility to this approach. Knowing what other people are doing, what they like, and giving them a forum to tell others, is one of the most powerful forms of influence imaginable. And as you are automatically grouping people by similar interests, they help each other... but they are not hawking the product too blatantly. This is superpromoting in action-satisfied customers, higher sales...

This particular way of managing the behavior of people to encourage them to make recommendations still has a lot of mileage left in it. The models used to provide you with carefully managed information are becoming ever more sophisticated. Gekko.com, for example, *"...recommends hotels and restaurants that are spot on for you. Find and book the right place by matching your preferences with like-minded people in the Gekko community."* On a worldwide basis, no less!

Consumers clearly want these types of recommendations. Since there is way too much wood for the trees. By gently, unobtrusively, offering them the option of following the herd's comparable choice, the stress of making a choice is removed and the purchasing decision more easily made.

2. Organized Word-of-mouth: Much has already been written about the organized form of word of mouth. It is all about the art of stimulating recommendations by *product seeding*. The principle has taken on new dimensions and sophistication from the days when Nike was handing out its footwear to the coolest boys and girls at school. Companies such as Buzzer[43], Bzzagent and Tremor (part of Procter & Gamble) are all specialists in this area. They work with a database of customers who like to try out new products and services and share their opinions about them with others. By offering these people the chance to experience a new product, they are encouraged to speak to their friends and social circle about it and report back on what they have learned. They also like to pass along free samples they've received to friends to try as well, all in an effort to speed up natural dissemination by word of mouth that might happen under "natural" circumstances. The art lies in trying to strike a balance between the natural processes by which ideas spread on one side, and the organized stimulation of word-of-mouth behavior on the other. Now called *Buzzers*, these people are not given any money for trying out new products but are given a free hand in what they wish to say about the products they are *buzzing* – this should make their recommendations more sincere and believable. When people's word of mouth is paid for they belong to the next category, paid endorsement.

3. Paid Endorsement: The least sincere method of producing word of mouth is by paid endorsement. The endorser tells people to buy/try a product because he has a commercial interest in doing so. It follows the same dynamic as a salesperson in a shop who is recommending something to you because he wants to sell it to you: enthusiasm may be a small part of it, but is not the primary driver. In fact, the more enthusiastic the salesperson is, or appears to be, the better they are doing their job. It might persuade people to contribute, but the commercial nature of the relationship can distort and bias the response.

The influence of word-of-mouth marketing is becoming more apparent to businesses every day. As a result most companies with a sales and marketing program are actively pursuing these strategies. Although well adopted it remains difficult to manage. Some companies have tried to enlist consumers into their ranks by offering a reward for their recommendations. Consumers are being paid to tell their friends and acquaintances to buy a given product. However, if the consumer is only making these recommendations based on the money they are getting, the whole thing can quickly become a little obvious. It doesn't feel right. People are being paid to do something they should be doing spontaneously. If it is too obvious that the recommendation is only the result of the monetary incentive, the promoter's reputation will suffer, and ultimately, so will that of the product, brand or company. There are well-known examples of companies paying students to post positive reactions on blogs about products. When things like this are discovered the company runs a real risk of doing serious damage to its reputation. The superpromoters of such companies in particular will be disappointed when these things come to light. Just think about it... After the "scam" has been exposed, if someone posts a genuine and enthusiastic comment on a blog, it will always smell suspicious. Trust in the company could suffer long-term damage. It's particularly damaging, as people nowadays want authenticity and sincere enthusiasm. Their trust is not for sale.

Having said this, there are other ways to make good use of paid endorsement. Businesses have been attracting sports heroes and other celebrities for centuries (was the earliest form, "By Appointment to his Majesty..."?) to tout their wares. It works, psychologists tell us, because people like to emulate their role models and will copy their behavior. Provided their recommendation comes across as believable.

If the celebrity does not manage to convince people because somehow the product doesn't fit with them, or the brand doesn't match the personality, there will be little or no effect from the endorsement.

There are yet other ways of using paid endorsement to your advantage. Magazines have been rewarding their subscribers for years with discounts or coupons if they recommend new subscribers. These rewards are sufficiently modest for it is not worthwhile to be pushing something they aren't actually enthusiastic about anyway. Since the magazine is still being recommended because of sincere enthusiasm, this form of paid endorsement only serves to smoothen a fairly natural word-of-mouth process. The primary motivation is enthusiasm, not money.

Another tried and true example of paid endorsement, successful since 1946, comes in the form of Tupperware parties. Tupperware assists their independent consultants in organizing an at-home party for friends and neighbors, where people come to see and try Tupperware products. It is not difficult to imagine what is being talked about most at a Tupperware party. The host, or traditionally, hostess, receives a commission on sales, making her performance a partially purchased one. However, the fact that this marketing concept has proven to be such a success for such a long time suggests that the limits of believability were not exceeded. The hostess's environment accepted it.

But if the reward is not transparent to everyone, the paid endorsement strategy can be fraught with danger. At the very least, if it is all in the open, the consumer can decide for himself whether or not to be influenced by the paid-for message.

Expanding influence

In this section we will be taking a look at the means and ways of expanding the influence of a superpromoter. Many companies in developing their sales techniques use their knowledge of social influencing. The principles of influencing behavior are a pillar of sales training seminars. One way of exercising influence on consumers happens when businesses communicate with customers directly. Advertising, brochures, catalogs and websites all exist for no other reason than to influence consumers directly. They do not exist to encourage customer-to-customer influencing: we'd call that word of mouth. In fact, how customers exercise influence on each other is a little understood area with many unknowns for most companies. Some companies have been experimenting with creating communities where customers can have direct communication with others. This encourages social sharing within the community, while the company can follow all that is happening at its source.

It is not wise for a company to try to manage the natural communication between customers too much. They can remove obstacles to a customer's positive input, perhaps when the benefits of a product are difficult to explain. Take Twitter, for example. It is quite hard to explain the value of messages posted in SMS language on a website in order to inform others of your basically trivial activities. Twitter could support the – otherwise very impressive – inroads their service is making by assisting Twitter superpromoters in explaining its value to others. There is no need to seek the enthusiasm of *natural* early adopters of these types of new technologies, they are usually curious enough to try new things out before all of its benefits are understood. Part of their motivation comes from the pleasure of trying out something new. It will be more difficult to persuade other people who are less eager to try out new communication tools. If, however, twittering superpromoters were handed a short but clear message to use for this purpose, it would no doubt be used to influence the people in their social circle.

Expanding the weapons of influence

Superpromoters, we have seen, are taken seriously when they come across as reliable, and if they have relevant information to impart. Companies can assist their super-promoters in coming across in a reliable manner by making sure they are themselves consistent. If it is clear what the business is doing and where it is going, it is also easier for superpromoters to endorse what the company stands for. If it is hard to support the policies a company has taken, it is also harder for the superpromoters to be consistent. Turning this way and that to defend the company, telling a story they might not be sure about, is not going to persuade superpromoters to stay on track. Time, then, to make sure that the superpromoters know what's going on, what the strategic and tactical choices are that the company is making. Better, yet, to have the superpromoter join in and help your thinking. Two birds, one stone ... Your superpromoters are giving you valuable input and they get the information they need to explain what's going on to their social circle.

In this regard, the more relevant information is made available to the superpromoter, the more their influence expands. This is another relatively easy way for a company to support its superpromoters. A very effective method is to provide superpromoters with advance information; super-promoters' egos are well massaged if they can tell everyone in their circle when tickets are going on sale, or how to get a special discount.

One way or the other, superpromoters are appealing to other people; this exerts an influence on their environment, which is not to be underestimated. Companies can make use of this when they are planning to influence certain target groups. The principles of attraction are as old as the hills (older, perhaps?) and the advertising industry knows very well how physical attraction can influence consumers. Seeking the support of superpromoters can make the most of this principle since all of them see enthusiasm as an attractive characteristic. Finally, superpromoters will know exactly what is considered appealing to their social circle. This could be sports heroes or pop celebrities, but might just as easily be people from their immediate environment. This type of information can then be used for marketing and communication purposes.

Expanding the superpromoter's armory is one way of expanding their influence; making the world more receptive toward their enthusiasm is another. Their influence can only take on exponential growing strength once their social environment is ready. If it is not ready yet, the company has either to be satisfied with fewer customers, or must try to encourage the superpromoter's social circle to become more receptive.

Getting the Superpromoter's network ready

What should a company do to expand the susceptibility of the superpromoter's social network? No single answer exists to that question. But creative marketing folk will surely get some good ideas by studying their superpromoters and the ways in which they interact with their social networks. It has become much easier to study social networks since the advent of the internet. By studying the structure of superpromoters' social networks, it is possible to determine whether the greater challenge lies with influencing the superpromoter's circle of close friends, or with influencing the periphery of his social network. When networks come in the form of a Small World Network, the chances for a rapid spread of enthusiasm will be greatest. Yet, if their immediate relationships are too close, we must encourage the superpromoter to move in other social circles as well. On the other hand, if the ties are too loose, the superpromoter must be assisted in developing closer ties. Companies can facilitate this by organizing events and moderating online meetings.

Once we understand the network's structure and the superpromoter has told us what his social circle is ready for, we are then ready to plan and implement a focused marketing and communication plan. A new landscape opens up before us, and the path is not easy to find, but marketers who discover the way will rule the land and have the best results.

Gut feeling

The Odilia method offers much information that can be put to work immediately. But we cannot do without the gut feel of marketing people or entrepreneurs themselves. We need their gut feelings to start offering more creative support to superpromoters. It's probably true that we will never fully fathom a superpromoter's psychology and, what's more, it's something that's always changing. Although we only get occasional glimpses of pieces of that puzzle, slowly but surely, the full picture is emerging. This is thanks in no small part to what superpromoters are teaching us! In offering support to superpromoters it's vital that gut feelings and creativity are brought to bear. We need to provide the ideas that nobody yet has thought of to stimulate their enthusiasm. When this happens we can give birth to new products and new ways of doing our marketing and communicating. It's when new superpromoters are born and their enthusiasm nurtured and fed. It's when businesses and consumers develop closer ties. It's when people working in companies relearn how to become as enthusiastic as their customers about their products. It's the end of the world as we know it and the beginning of something more beautiful.

IN CONCLUSION . . . AND PEEKING FORWARD

In this chapter we discovered who Odilia is and how she works. Using the Odilia method you can get to work with your superpromoters tomorrow, starting with an orientation of existing information and a definition of who the superpromoters are that you want to focus on. Then you invite them in and listen to what they have to say. To interpret their feedback properly, it is useful to have some understanding of the origins of enthusiasm, the ways in which it is transferred and which factors are involved in influence. Finally, the structure of social networks must be understood. When we have a good understanding of our superpromoter, we can offer them our support by feeding their enthusiasm, encouraging its spread through their social circle, and hence, expanding their influence.

The next and last chapter will talk about how we can change the world if we allow ourselves to be led by our superpromoters.

6

IT'S THE END OF THE WORLD AS WE KNOW IT

INTRODUCTION[44]

We are about to begin the last chapter of *The Superpromoter*, so let's hope, having made it this far, that you've become just as enthusiastic about superpromoters as I have. When you actually meet a few of them who are really enthusiastic about something that's relevant to you, there's always a good chance you'll be struck by their enthusiasm too. It is a really worthwhile exercise for any kind of organization to track down its superpromoters, to support them in what they're doing, and to travel down the road together. This sound advice applies as much to commercial businesses as it does to government agencies...to the largest multinational enterprises and to the corner-shop; after all, both can have superpromoters as customers. These organizations should stop their excessive focus on unhappy, discontented customers. Instead, they ought to be discovering who their superpromoters are and start listening to them. Those organizations that understand their superpromoters well and work with them the right way have the greatest opportunity to outsail their competition. In fact, with a superpromoter on board, you could end up charting a "course to the deep blue ocean where demand is created rather than fought over" in entirely new markets, with no competition on the horizon at all.[45]

When an organization succeeds in shifting its focus to its superpromoters, this implies a radical departure from the way in which customers will be approached from then on. In this brave new world, superpromoters are given an important role to play during new product development and in the communication of those new products to the outside world. Here, they become a sounding board whose critical comments and suggestions carry impressive weight. For the brave new company, criticism coming from their superpromoters' board would go straight to the heart and be taken as seriously as criticism from Board Members and Shareholders. All of this represents an entirely new way of understanding the world...it heralds the end of existing paradigms...

THE END OF PRODUCT DEVELOPMENT AS WE KNOW IT

New product development is ideally suited for the role that superpromoters could play in our new world order. If they don't like it, there's not much of a chance out there, either. Without the support of your superpromoters, you can forget about your chances of a successful new launch. The best strategy in new product development therefore is to ensure the support of your superpromoters by seeking their involvement *ab ovo*. The first way of doing this is to have them try out new products for you. Even better is to have superpromoters participate directly in thinking up new product ideas. Other superpromoters can then be involved in deciding whether the idea is a hit or miss. A nice example of what we're talking about can be found at *Designme. com*. Designers can post their ideas for the design of a new product or an improvement to an existing product on the site. Other designers get to judge their design. This is a fine way of having the best ideas float to the surface.

When you've got your superpromoters involved in the design process the chances that something will be a hit are far greater than when new product ideas are handed down from an ivory R&D tower. R&D would be better off supporting the co-creation process, evaluating, for example, the technical feasibility of new ideas, and their financial viability. There's no doubt that products which have been co-created by superpromoters will be greatly approved of by their superpromoting peers, but the added punch comes from the fact that their social circle are likely to approve as well. From the superpromoter's perspective, their social circle is always looking over their shoulders; so anything they are working on will be in equal parts created with them in mind. Anything created in this way has the potential of becoming a runaway success. Whether a superpromoter had a hand in the creation of something new or not, it is in any event quite essential to have their input in determining its market potential.

Why are superpromoters so good as co-creators?

... They are willing
... They are knowledgeable
... They like to share their opinions
... They are creative
... They have social intelligence
... They like to be influential
... They understand their social surroundings

THE END OF MARKETING AS WE KNOW IT

The discipline of Marketing has evolved to be quite complex. Not only are consumers being overwhelmed with information, but there are also an ever-increasing number of message transmitters at work vying for their attention and trying to influence them. As a result, a new generation of media-savvy consumers has evolved which is much harder to influence by commercial messages. Their attention has become an elusive quarry for marketers to stalk. Fortunately, there is one group of customers that a company can reach. Superpromoters are interested in the products made by companies they are enthusiastic about, and will sit up and take notice when these companies make contact.

If a company doesn't factor its superpromoters into the equation when orchestrating its mass communication they risk losing out twice. If the message does not relate to them personally superpromoters may feel marginalized. Particularly, if they were under the impression that they had a special and unique relationship with the company, who now is just talking to the masses without consulting them. This will dampen their enthusiasm and weaken their tendency to speak in positive terms about the brand. The unintentional result of mass communication is that it upsets the superpromoter's enthusiasm and inhibits its dissemination. Not feeling addressed by the message, the superpromoter will be less willing to fulfill their promoting role. The rest of the consumer world doesn't pay much attention to mass communication from a company they don't feel close ties to anyway. They would probably prefer instead to listen to superpromoters. This is the second way a company can lose out.

Mass communication only makes sense if it makes superpromoters enthusiastic and actively supports the dissemination of their enthusiasm. The smartest marketers by now have understood where to concentrate their energies. There are two ways available to them. The first is to focus their marketing effort directly at superpromoters and to support them while they are busy doing what they do best: influencing their social surroundings. The second is to use a slightly adapted mass communication strategy. The adapted strategy should be designed to appeal to a superpromoter, while simultaneously helping to make the rest of the world more receptive to the superpromoter's message. Ideally, the mass communication should help superpromoters in talking to their network or support their message in other meaningful ways.

THE END OF MARKET RESEARCH AS WE KNOW IT

Market research has always sought to perform the same function. It is to form a representative picture of the opinions of consumers and business customers. The same statistical tools have been used to this end for the last 50 yeas. With these tools we can describe the opinions of the average customer without needing to go out and interview every one as we can now achieve this by means of a representative sample. When, however, marketing and product development is being aimed at superpromoters, you no longer need a representative picture. Who cares about the average customer? The statistical method used to present an average customer is not at all suited to capture a superpromoter.[46] New research needs to concentrate on the

superpromoter and the complexity of enthusiasm, its transfer and social influencing. This new and exiting research
area has strong links to social psychology and sociology.
Market researchers have to focus their knowledge and talent on understanding the superpromoter and must be
open to try new ways. New methods are needed to identify
copycat and herd behavior and to render the subconscious
processes more visible. They must develop techniques to
understand the emotional components of enthusiasm. This
subtle, yet huge shift heralds a move away from the simple
process of collecting opinions and introduces social knowledge as the key research goal. Superpromoters aren't mere
respondents to your survey; they are market researchers in
their own right. Their ability to map the landscape stems
from their keen understanding of their social surroundings. How exactly a social environment can be susceptible
to influence by enthusiasm is the *Ultima Thule* for market
researchers. Enough said for now...

THE END OF MANAGEMENT AS WE KNOW IT

A while back we discussed the thought that superpromoters are in a sense the guardians of an organization's soul.
Entrepreneurs start up businesses because they are the ultimate superpromoters of their products. When they start their
business, they are enthusiastic about their product and plan
to conquer all markets with it. All it takes is one superpromoter, in the shape of an entrepreneur, to ignite the spark
that gives birth to a new enterprise. When superpromoting
customers can be found, that spark bursts into flame; let's
hope its wildfire! If the entrepreneur remains true to their

original dream they will continue to make products about which they are as enthusiastic as that first one they ever made. Customers and employees who share this enthusiasm resemble the entrepreneur in more ways than one. Whether consciously or subconsciously they all share a similar passion. In start-up companies the founder is a superpromoter who listens carefully to other superpromoters. As companies take off and grow, there is always the unfortunate tendency for contact between the original superpromoter and their clients to diminish. Once this happens there's a risk that the business has peaked and success will be sliding downhill from there on in. If companies become aware of this, the thing for them to do is to concentrate all of their management skills on their best friends: the superpromoters. If Boards, Directors and current management of the business don't meet superpromoter criteria, it's time to clear the decks and make way for new ones who do.

Because the day of the Superpromoter has arrived!

It's the End of the World as We Know It

...*And I Feel Fine*

POSTSCRIPT

My deadline is one day off as I am writing this...the book, my book, seems to be about finished...about to become your book, the reader's. Just a few more words, a few corrections, add in the latest research material, finish this postscript and it can go to the editor. As of tomorrow it won't be mine anymore...decidedly an odd realization.

This is the second time I've written a book. The previous one was a collection of poetry. Slowly, I am beginning to understand how the same problem I had then is recurring this time. For writers their book is never finished. A poem isn't the only thing you keep on tinkering with; the same surely applies to *The Superpromoter*. Every day brings new ideas and fresh insights. They come from new research results, from talking to clients or to people at work, or just from something that happened. There's so much to discover and learn!

It is not an option, however, to wait until the superpromoters have revealed all their secrets. As if you could discover them all...It must be the same as trying to find out everything there is to know about your partner, friends or even yourself: impossible. There is always something new to discover. Just as well, really, it's what keeps it interesting.

As for me, I'm very happy that I got to know the superpromoter. They've been around during the last year or so and were a continuous source of inspiration. It's not very often that ideas and insights were coming to me as fast as they did during this period. My epiphany was to start seeing the world through different eyes; I now see us surrounded by enthusiastic friends; people who mean us well. During the past several years I have had the privilege of introducing companies in every industry imaginable to their superpromoting friends. Sometimes it made me feel as if I brought their long lost son back home to them...their superpromoter was welcomed with open arms and offered the best hospitality the house had to offer. It is gratifying to be this type of messenger: not the one who tells them what to improve, but the bringer of the good news that their company can be seriously proud of what they do. What? Making their customers so enthusiastic that even their environment catches the buzz of their excitement.

A great number of the statements I make in *The Superpromoter* are based on surveys conducted among thousands of consumers, while others are based on several observations. Then there are also some statements on these pages that anticipate the results of future research. It seems clear to me that there is ample evidence that proves the influence of infectious enthusiasm on any company's success. And on our personal development as well! Sometimes the evidence is marshaled by indirect routes, such as when I refer to other books and articles, while on other occasions the experiments are woven together in order to arrive at new insights. The fundamental scientists among us will not always approve of this methodology, yet *The Superpromoter* shouldn't be seen as a doctoral thesis, or its commercialized offshoot. For me, it has always been a vision, one that I sought to provide with solid underpinnings. But it is also an invitation to search for new evidence, including evidence that could disprove some of the statements I have made here. That kind of evolution is good; it will not invalidate the importance of the superpromoter. The force of enthusiasm force is unmistakably present.

The idea that superpromoters exist is based on any number of supporting theories, some of which have been around for more that 50 years. It means that this is more than just some new and untried idea coming along, and *The Superpromoter* owes a debt of gratitude to many sources. Having said that, there is still a great deal more for us to discover; this journey has only just begun! Perhaps the best way to look at *The Superpromoter* is as a crossroads for ideas to meet and mingle and then continue on their separate journeys with fresh energy. I certainly hope over the coming years to learn a good amount more about superpromoters and their friends. For me, this love affair is far from over.

If I have succeeded in what I set out to do in writing this book, I will have handed you a lens that brings the force of enthusiasm into sharp focus. Please don't put that lens aside when you lay aside *The Superpromoters*! You have superpromoters waiting for you.

They'll be disappointed if you don't accept their invitation....

A THANK YOU TO MY
SUPERPROMOTERS

Here, at the end of this journey, I would like to offer my thanks to all of my superpromoters who made it possible for me to offer you these ideas. They played three important roles that attentive readers of *The Superpromoter* should be able to recognize by now: they were my coach, my motivator and my source of inspiration. A special thanks for the people who helped publishing the English Edition. Thanks to Peter de Wolff for his excellent translation. I am very thankful for the Blauw UK team, John Clarvis; Arthur Fletcher; Jonathan Wheeler; Henk Scholte for their proofreading and providing international content where the examples were too Dutch.

Thanks to my agent Bettina Querfurth for getting the book published in the UK and Germany, Eleanor Davey Corrigan for being my editor at Palgrave and the team at Newgen Imaging for co-creating the finishing touch with me. I thank Sophie Standaart en Maurice Kalis for being my assistants at Blauw.

I thank Mark Earls, Verne Harnish, Hans Böhm & Suhail Khan for their great endorsements and Patrick Lerou for helping me with this & supporting me from the first time we met!

Because of Jaap den Dulk it turned into a book that shows ambition. He dared to speak the truth, a truth that changed everything. Kees de Jong showed himself as the best kind of superpromoter you could wish for when, unannounced, he wrote a column in praise of the superpromoter in *The Dutch Financial Times* and showed himself as a most valuable coach. Ton Otker manfully struggled through several versions and managed to stay available as a crystal clear sounding board throughout. My tried and true mentor, Willem Bosveld, was there for me at every twist and turn in the road, offering me the sustenance I needed for the trip. Pieter Willems offered me extensive and well thought-out feedback, all the while encouraging me to be even stricter than I thought possible. Jorrit Lang was not just one of my best readers, he also proved himself a worthy opponent during our joint performances in Rotterdam and Barcelona, among other places. Rene Gerhardus was quick as a blade and sharp as one, too; he cut to the core and gave me pause to reflect. Wiggert de Haan challenged me to make my story more personal and to make up my mind to play the role of expert. Willem Sodderland, who hails from the world of organized recommendations, supplied his endless expertise. Mark Hesseling was another one of the readers; motivated as researcher, but also as friend. My brother Ton and my father, Hans, were readers of my manuscript who shed their own light on my ideas. Harry Scholte urged me to be clearer, while Marc Verkuijl read with the perspective of an IT expert. Robert van Ossenbruggen offered some of his wonderful insight just in time and for a while Maarten Veeger lent me his journalist's eye. Dimitri Kruik supplied a fresh perspective from the financial point of view. Walter Vesters, Jacques Cools and Peter Rikhof from Scope Business Media offered a fantastic stage and the warmest of welcomes during their lunches with Ron Blaauw. My publisher, Ina

Boer deserves my sincere thanks for her trust as well as her belief that we were on to something good, right from the start. Sophieke Thurmer deserves plaudits for her role as editor and help as a sounding board.

Sandra Bosma at Blauw Research trawled through immense amounts of data to bring pearls to the surface. Maike van Breda added important nuances to the flow of the story. Operating from several perspectives, Thao Nguyen analyzed the NPS, Copy Cat and Herd Behavior as well as The Smart Subconscious. Babs Asselbergs contributed her expertise in customer research while looking over my shoulder. Coming from the practical side of things, Claartje Jansen contributed, among much else, her NPS experience. Hidde Moerman found a superpromoter in the Dutch town of Apeldoorn. Wout Thuis, Isabelle Horner, Peter Dost, Karin Totté, Gaby Remmers and Bobbie van Beest built up the first version with their solid input. Bastian Verdel brought his thinking cap from Germany, while Nils Knoot's assistance improved the structure. Ilona Weydeveld schot the first superpromoter film clips. Jurian Meijering and Noortje Wijnstok developed the connection between the superpromoter and reputation research. Keete Kruijtzer, Nienke Vreugdenhil, Marlies Kerklaan, Manon Barten-ten Haaf, Jan Hendrik de Groot and Sylvie Verbiest all starred as superpromoters in the clips, each making their own very personal contributions. Marco de Groot had a contribution to make from the public sector. Bart Roozen contributed enthusiasm; his own. Dori van Rosmalen also shot a large number of superpromoter film clips. Tamara Vijverberg got the Ministry of Home Affairs to be enthusiastic and tracked down superpromoters on the web. Maarten Sentjes shot film and then edited it down to its essential core. Sonja Vernooij and Ine Armour-Brown offered themselves as sounding boards based on their expertise with qualitative research. René de Man looked at the superpromoter in sponsor surveys. Olivier Hendriks, Kim Derrix, Rini Haverlag and Carmen Bogers helped me with presentations for several clients. Wendy Loorbach-van Zutphen and Caroline Nevens went through the latest version of the manuscript with a fine-toothed comb in search of spelling gremlins. Jochem Meijer, Binne Heida and Ivo Langbroek identified the first superpromoters during research, while Michelle de Laat and Menno Urbanus validated the concept. They were helped by their colleagues from P&D and BlauwNL who played an essential role, as they did in all of the research work. Maaike Wentink turned out additional analyses and Tessa Belt scoured the Good Housekeeping Fair in Amsterdam in search of superpromoters. Eva Gerritse, Willem Thomassen and Björn Terlouw took charge of the international validation. Elke Pool collected different formats in which questions were framed. Eelco van Dijk was making FMCC customers enthusiastic. Simone Nelissen, Anke Bergmans, Josine Poley and Ellen Ruitenberg went and analyzed superpromoters at the Dutch Railways. Arjen van Ulden designed the graphics and brochures. Erdinc Uskalelier created superpromoter questions for employees. Marielle Hobbelen's contribution helped our thinking about superpromoters among ethnic minorities. Froukje Schaaf combined the superpromoter with her insights gained from *The Wisdom of Crowds*. Annekatrien Bos kept an eye on newsletters that contained links to superpromoters. Amanda Haarman alerted us to Amsterdam trendwatcher and blogger Nalden. Xenia Hasker helped to build in our knowledge bank. Laurens Langendonck's contribution was quality management. Karin den Bouwmeester and Martje van der Linde brought expertise from Delft's University of Technology and Eline Driesen did a fine job photoshopping me into Superman for an ad. Henk Scholte challenged me to write a new preface. Wout van der Wijk first announced his enthusiasm for the manuscript in an SMS, adding his verbal feedback soon after. Frank, Jos, Els and Bram brought their ideas from Blauw's MT. Jos Vink also came up with www.superpromotersvanblauw.nl, which became our entry for the MOAwards and rewarded us with a Research Company of the year 2009 award. The superpromoter team helped me to build Odilia, where Bauke Aukema and Pepijn Sitter brought their expertise to bear on the results. Jos Verduijn and Stephan Kusters designed www.superpromoter.nl. Then there are a number of internship trainees who deserve to be mentioned for their analytical work and research: Heleen Bovenkerk, Laura Straeter, Dirk Korbijn, Sandra van de Kooij, Sjoerd Prins and Kristian Bolk, thanks for all your efforts! Finally, I'd like to thank everyone at *Blauw* for creating such an inspiring environment for me to work in. Anybody I forgot to mention...I beg your forgiveness right now. I'll put that right in the next edition, just as soon as I find out!

However, before I can conclude my words of thanks, I should like to offer my deepest gratitude to Nicole Remmers, both as reader of my work and as my wife, and surely also for her smiling patience, required to cope with my stream-of-consciousness flow of ideas. Finally, I am not forgetting that I owe her more than thanks for letting me be absent, physically and mentally, for so much of the time.

My two sons, Loek and Guus, deserve my gratefulness thank you for their pure and unconditional enthusiasm.

ABOUT THE AUTHOR

Born in 1969 in a southern region of the Netherlands, Rijn Vogelaar graduated from secondary school in 1988, where he had met his first superpromoter. This was Philip Verdult, his Dutch teacher who had kind things to say about his poetry.

His degrees from the University of Amsterdam, in social psychology and psychological methodology, preceded his post graduate research work in "Personal Relevance, Elaboration and Choice Behaviour" at Leeds University. While in England, he toured the country as "adopted poet" with a band, *Lemonade*. During his student days, Rijn was a research assistant to Dr. Willem Bosveld, during which time two publications saw the light of day:

Bosveld, W., Koomen, W. & Vogelaar, R. (1997). "Construing a Social Issue: Effects on Attitudes and the False Consensus Effect", *British Journal of Social Psychology*, 36, pp. 263 – 272.

Bosveld, W., Vogelaar, R. & Koomen, W. (1994). Differentiële representaties van een complex onderwerp: Dezelfde mening over verschillende situaties, in Ellemers, N., Van der Kloot, W., De Vries, N.K. & Buunk, A.P. (Eds.). *Fundamentele Sociale Psychologie*, deel 8. Tilburg University Press.

After graduation he fulfilled his military service as an applied researcher in the Social Sciences Department of the Dutch

Royal Navy, followed by an assignment at the department of behavioral sciences of the Royal Dutch Armed Forces, and thereafter as labor markets researcher and policy advisor at the Ministry of Defence.

In 2000, he published a collection of his poetry in, *De Euforie van wankel evenwicht* [The Euphoria of an Unstable Balance], with Gopher Publishers.

Since 2000 Rijn has been working at *Blauw Research*; partner since 2004 and General Director since January of 2008.

Rijn is married to Nicole Remmers and is the father of two sons, Loek (2006) and Guus (2009).

MORE INFORMATION

More information about superpromoters can be found at www.superpromoters.com. The site contains a wide range of filmclips about superpromoters from many different categories of business, and life. Research results are posted here, and the site also has a blog to accomodate the flow of ideas about superpromoters. All of our new thinking about superpromoters will be recorded here as well.

If you would like support in getting to know super-promoters, please contact us at *Blauw Research*. It is likely that we already know quite a bit about your particular superpromoters!

Blauw Research
Weena 125
3013 CK Rotterdam
Tel. ++10 4000900
Mail. info@blauw.com
Or visit: www.blauw.com

If you would like to get in touch with the author, please send your mail to rijn.vogelaar@superpromoters.com

NOTES

1. In his autobiographical book, *Ver heen* [Far Gone], the author, P.C. Kuiper offers a description of his experience with depression. To Kuiper, who is a professor of psychiatry, the moment in time when he felt he had emerged from his depression was when he first started to enjoy music again (P.C. Kuiper, *Ver heen. Verslag van een depressie.* SDU, Den Haag 1988).

2. One well-known book on this topic would be *Authenticity* by James H. Gillmore & B. Joseph Pine, Harvard Business School Press, 2007. The authors indicate that the perception of authenticity is of great importance to the appeal of a brand.

3. *Blue Ocean Strategy*, W. Chan Kim & Reneé Mauborgne, Harvard Business School Press, 2005.

4. *Herd: How to Change Mass Behaviour by Harnessing Our True Nature*, Mark Earls, John Wiley & Sons Ltd, 2007.

5. www.exactitudes.com gives you a clear picture of the ways people copy each other.

6. *Het Slimme Onbewuste* [The Smart Subconscious], Ap Dijksterhuis, Bert Bakker, 2007.

7. Cialdini, R.B. (2001), Influence: Science and Practice (4th ed.), Boston: Allyn & Bacon.

8. Milgram, S. (1963), "Behavioral Study of Obedience", *Journal of Abnormal and Social Psychology*, 67, pp. 371–378.

9. *The Long Tail*, Chris Anderson, Random House Business Books, 2007.

10. *The Tipping Point*, Malcolm Gladwell, Little Brown, 2000.

11. *Unleashing the Ideavirus*, Seth Godin, 2001; *Diffusion of Innovations*, Everett M. Rogers, Free Press, 2003; Emanuel Rosen, *The Anatomy of Buzz Revisited*, Doubleday, 2009.

12. *We are Smarter Than Me: How to Unleash the Power of Crowds on Your Business*, Barry Libert & Jon Spector, Wharton School Publishing, 2008.

13. www.http://mindstorms.lego.com

14. Slogan used for the NL Conference 2008.

15. This case is described extensively in *Coca-Cola, l'enquête interdite*, William Reymond, Flammarion, 2006.

16. *Advocacy Drives Growth: Customer Advocacy Drives UK Business Growth, 2005,* by Dr. Paul Marsden and Alain Samson of the London School of Economics's Institute of Social Psychology and Neville Upton, chief executive of The Listening Company.

17. See also, *The Discipline of Market Leaders: Choose Your Customers, Narrow Your Focus, Dominate Your Market*, by Michael Treacey & Fred Wiersema, Perseus Books, 1995.

18. From, *Whale done!: The Power of Positive Relationships*, by Kenneth Blanchard, Free Press, 2002.

19. Theodore Leavitt, *Marketing Myopia*, Harvard Business Review, 1960.

20. Fred Reichheld; *The Ultimate Question: Driving Good Profits and True Growth*, Boston: Harvard Business Press, 2006.

21. Article in progress, Drs. Sandra Bosma (Blauw Research) and Frank H.M. Verbeeten MBA (RSM Erasmus University).

22. In *Good to Great*, Jim Collins shows us companies that have been successful for decades because they have never lost sight of the soul of their organization and have remained loyal to it. *Good to Great*, Jim Collins, Collins, 2001.

23. *The Wisdom of Crowds*, James Surowiecky, Doubleday, 2004.

24. See also, *No Budget Marketing*, Jos Burgers, Academic Service, Sdu Uitgevers, 2006.

25. "NET PROMOTER®, NPS® and NET PROMOTER SCORE® are registered trademarks of Satmetrix Systems, Inc., F. Reichheld, and Bain & Company, Inc."

26. Reichheld, F., "The One Number you Need to Grow", *Harvard Business Review*, Dec. 2003, pp. 46–54.

27. *The Loyalty Effect*, Fred. Reichheld, HBS Press, 1996.

28. *Loyalty Rules*, Fred. Reichheld, HBS Press, 2001.

218

29. In *Answering the Ultimate Question*, Laura Brooks and Richard Owen offer a number of pragmatic reference points to assist the reader in establishing the proper relationship between NPS® and sales growth. *Answering the Ultimate Question*, Richard Owen & Laura L. Brooks, Jossey Bass, 2009.

30. These scores are very much product or industry-dependent. In some industries a net score greater than zero, even in North America, is already quite a respectable performance.

31. These conferences are organized by Satmetrix and are held annually in London and in the US. They are instructive because many attendees share experiences on implementing customer relationship measurements and the role the NPS® can perform.

32. This principle is given an elegant description in *The Long Tail* by Chris Anderson, Random House Business Books, 2007.

33. Ton Otker & Harm van Leeuwen, WOM, Research World, September 2006.

34. Article in progress, Drs. Sandra Bosma (Blauw Research) and Frank H.M. Verbeeten MBA (RSM Erasmus University).

35. Reichheld, F., "The One Number you Need to Grow", *Harvard Business Review*, Dec. 2003, pp. 46–54.

36. Timothy L. Keiningham, Bruce Cooil, Tor Wallin Andreassen & Lerzan Aksoy, "A Longitudinal Examination of Net Promoter and Firm Revenue Growth", *Journal of Marketing*, vol.71 (July 2007), pp. 39–51.
    Keiningham T.L., Cooil B., Aksoy L., Andreassen T.W. & Weiner J. (2007), "The Value of Different Customer Satisfaction & Loyalty Metrics in Predicting Customer Retention, Recommendation, and Share-of-Wallet", *Managing Service Quality*, vol. 17, no. 4, pp. 361–384.

37. We have discussed before how original behavior turns out to be copied behavior as well, merely coming from a less obvious source.

38. S.E. Asch published his findings in several articles, including, Asch, S.E. (1951). "Effects of Group Pressure upon the Modification and Distortion of Judgment", in H. Guetzkow (ed.) *Groups, Leadership and Men*. Pittsburgh, PA: Carnegie Press. Also, Asch, S.E. (1955). *Opinions and Social Pressure*, Scientific American, 193, pp. 31–35

39. *Het Slimme Onbewuste* [The Smart Subconscious], Ap Dijksterhuis, Bert Bakker, 2007.

40. www.Superpromoters.com, Trollbeads.

41. In *Six Degrees*, Duncan Watts describes the complexity of a social network and how its structure and flammability ensure that viruses and ideas will spread. *Six Degrees: The Science of a Connected Age,* Duncan J. Watts, Norton, 2003.

42. Mark S. Granovetter, "The Strenght of Weak Ties", *American Journal of Sociology*, vol. 78, no. 6 (May 1973), pp. 1360–1380.

43. More information can be found at www.buzzer.nl

44. Lyrics from *It's the End of the World as We Know It* by an American rock band called R.E.M.

45. *Blue Ocean Strategy*, W. Chan Kim & Reneé Mauborgne, Harvard Business School Press, 2005.

46. Superpromoters are better described by using Pareto's Power Law than by using the customary Bell-curve, normal to market research. In *Here Comes Everybody: the Power of Organizing without Organizations,* Clay Shirky and Allen Lane, 2008, fully describe the principle of the power law distribution.

INDEX